Welcome to Venice

Edmund and Jan Swinglehurst

Collins
Glasgow and London

Photographs
All photographs including cover by
Van Phillips
except the following:

pp. 114, 120, 122, J. Allan Cash
p. 93 Colour Library International
p. 121 Photobank
pp. 64 (btm), 95, 117, 118 Picturepoint
pp. 88, 104, 110 Spectrum
pp. 25, 91, 105 Edmund Swinglehurst
p. 64 Zefa

Illustrations
pp. 4—9 Peter Joyce

Maps
pp. 74—91 Marjorie and Reg Piggott
pp. 112—3 Mike Shand and Iain Gerard

Published 1987
Copyright © Edmund and Jan Swinglehurst 1987
Published by William Collins Sons and Company Limited
Printed in Great Britain

ISBN 0 00 447507 0

CONTENTS

HISTORY

The story of Venice begins in the fifth century with a frightened community on the mainland who were driven from their homes by Attila the Hun and his army of Barbarian invaders. For safety, the refugees set themselves up in the swampy islands of the Venetian lagoon and eventually created a highly civilized Empire of the Sea which lasted for centuries until the Napoleonic conquest of 1797.

In the first three centuries following their arrival in the Venetian lagoon, the new inhabitants lived separate lives in scattered communities along the shores of Malamocco (today's Lido) down by Chióggia and around Grado. Few of them settled in the Rialto islands which were regarded as too swampy and insect infested. Although there was little political unity among the earliest communities, a thread of common purpose dictated by the environment soon became evident. Deprived of agricultural land, the lagoon dwellers took to deriving a living from the sea by fishing, by the crystallization of sea salt and by boat building. Soon their skills at sea enabled them to sail up and down the coast offering a system of communication and trade with coastal towns.

While the mainland suffered the ravages of successive waves of invaders, including Goths, Ostrogoths, Lombards and Franks, the Venetians managed to survive relatively undisturbed, improving their boat building and navigational skills and developing techniques for the preservation, by salting, of the fish and game found in the lagoon.

From the early sixth century, Venice was a part of the Byzantine Empire, which had developed from the eastern Roman Empire, but by the ninth century Venice had developed a strong sense of its own individuality and independence.

The circumstances and shared environment of the refugees in these islands did not produce a unified social community but it did bring the people together in times of danger. Pepin, son of Charlemagne, took the mainland and set up his headquarters at Ravenna. He then attempted to invade the lagoon in 810 but the Venetians rallied together and, moving up to the Rialto islands for greater safety, repelled the Frankish force.

This event marked the beginning of the growth of the Republic of Venice on the Rialto islands. This central area, protected by water on all sides, was seen as a natural site for the headquarters of a community whose growing wealth and skill was beginning to come to the notice of other European nations. As a result of its wealth, Venice became a target for conquest by ambitious kings and barons.

Although they provided excellent refuge from intending invaders, the islands of the Rialto were even less suitable for building on than the sandy shores of Malamocco, Jesolo and Chióggia where most of the inhabitants lived in mud and wattle houses. To create foundations, the Venetians decided to sink a large number of tree trunks into the mud, so close together that they formed the solid platform on which the later stone palazzi were built and which still hold them up today.

As it grew and acquired an identity, Venice became more and more aware of the pressures exerted by the two great powers of the day, the Byzantine Empire

to the east and the Holy Roman Empire to the north. As members of the Byzantine Empire, the Venetians had certain trading rights in ports of the eastern Mediterranean and the Bosporus, but, as traders, they needed to remain on friendly terms with the Holy Roman Empire which controlled the trading routes into Europe. It was a dilemma that gave rise to rival factions in Venice and which caused the new Republic, in sympathy and self interest, to veer from one power to the other. In 811 their problem was resolved by a treaty between Charlemagne and the Byzantine Emperor, Nicophorus, in which it was agreed that Venice should be regarded as part of the Byzantine Empire but with a semi-independent status.

The sense of nationhood that was beginning to grow among the Venetians was sharpened still further when a Venetian ship brought the body of St Mark from Alexandria. Legend has it that St Mark's body was disinterred and smuggled out of Egypt in a barrel of salt pork, thereby discouraging a Moslem customs examination. The story is told in mosaic form on the south transept of St Mark's Basilica. St Mark now became the patron saint of Venice dislodging the former incumbent, St Theodore, whose statue still stands on a column of the Piazzetta by the Doge's Palace.

By 832 a church to the saint had already been consecrated on the ground now occupied by the Piazza S. Marco and the lion of St Mark was becoming a familiar sight on banners and ships of the Republic. In its new found status, and with the most powerful fleet in the Mediterranean, Venice now found itself courted by both the Holy Roman Empire and the Byzantines. The Roman Empire sought help from the Venetian fleet against the Slav pirates who were preying on shipping in the important Adriatic trade routes and help was also sought by the Byzantines against the Saracens who were crossing from Africa to harass Mediterranean shipping and to found colonies in Sicily and southern Italy.

The campaign against the pirates was a great success but the second, against the Saracens, was an unmitigated disaster. The Saracens sank the fleet sent to attack them and sailed impudently up the Adriatic as far as Ancona. The Venetians put the blame for the debacle on their Byzantine allies whom they accused of running away from the battle. In Venice, the faction in favour of alliance with the Holy Roman Empire, instead of the Byzantines, became more powerful.

This defeat by the Saracens was not the last which Venice was to suffer at the hands of an enemy but it did not restrict the continuing evolution of the Republic, nor did it weaken its resolve to protect itself against any enemy. As a result, when the Magyars swept down from Hungary into the valley of the Po and threatened Venice, the Venetians set about strengthening the defences of the Rialto Island by erecting a bastion that ran from the castle at the eastern end of the islands, across the Riva degli Schiavoni to the church of S. Maria (also known as S. Maria Zobenigo) del Giglio. From here, a heavy chain barrier was slung across the Canal Grande blocking its entry. Today, only a fraction of these formidable fortifications remains at the Rio del Arsenale.

Having dealt with the Magyar threat, the Venetians now faced a formidable enemy from the south — Robert Guiscard and his Norman army had arrived to take

over the lands previously occupied by the Saracens in Sicily and southern Italy. Guiscard's successes in Italy soon inspired him to attempt the conquest of the Byzantine Empire and once again the Byzantine Emperor called for Venetian help. Little persuasion was needed to bring the Venetian fleet to his aid as an enemy presence at the entry point to the Mediterranean threatened the trade routes which were the lifeline of the Republic of Venice.

By defeating the Normans and, thereby helping Byzantium as well as itself, Venice became very important. Before agreeing to defend Byzantium, the Venetians had extracted titles of honour and excellent trading rights from them. The Serenissima (or Serene Republic) as it was known, began to look even more like a world power.

The proclamation by Pope Urban II of the Crusades against the Saracens in 1095 threatened to disrupt the Venetian trade routes. There was an immediate response to the Pope's call from kings, barons, bishops and ordinary people whose enthusiasm was motivated by Christian ideology and more than a little self interest. Ever since the Arabs had invaded North Africa and Europe, bringing their advanced culture with them, rulers and the people of Europe had grown to appreciate the material benefits of Saracen culture. Moreover, they knew that the Holy Land was also the gateway and repository for trade with the Far East. Opportunities for plunder and trade were, therefore, immense.

The Venetians, whose links with the Saracens were of long standing, knew this and feared the effects of the arrival of ill-disciplined armies of opportunists on their so far exclusive business. On the other hand, as a Christian nation they could

hardly stand aside from the enthusiasm of all the rulers of Europe; so they procrastinated, preparing a fleet with uncharacteristic dilatoriness, while the Franks took Jerusalem and massacred the Saracens and the Jews.

Eventually the Venetians were ready to sail in 1097 but by this time the armies of Crusaders crossing Europe had grown to a flood of soldiers and vagabonds who lived off the land, pillaging villages and killing their fellow Christians as they went. In despair at this turn of events, the Byzantine Emperor called on the Venetians to drive off some of the Crusader fleets anchored off Byzantine ports; among these fleets were the Pisans who were becoming a thorn in the side of Venetian traders. The Venetians welcomed the opportunity to deal with the Pisans and, changing course, they succeeded in catching them at Rhodes where they captured 20 of their ships and 4000 prisoners before proceeding to the Holy Land.

Here they were welcomed by the victorious Franks who were in urgent need of maritime support and they offered the Venetians extensive trading rights in return for their help.

To raise money for these new enterprises, the Venetian Great Council, which had gradually limited the personal power of the Doge, now divided Venice into six districts, or *sestieri*, in order to facilitate the collection of taxes. With the money thus collected, Venice increased its ship building industry and the size of its fleets and by the time of the Fourth Crusade in 1202 she was able to contribute 480 of her own ships to a campaign that was not entirely to her liking. The strategy of the Fourth Crusade had been devised by Richard the Lion-Heart, whose plan for

the defeat of the Saracens included an attack on Egypt — a country with which the Venetians had only recently made extensive trading agreements.

There now occurred one of those devious manipulations at which the Venetians were masters. At the time, the Venetian Doge was Enrico Dandolo who was 90 years old and almost blind. Dandolo accompanied the Crusaders and managed to persuade them that it was a justifiable aim of the Crusade to attack Constantinople on the way to the Holy Land. Some of the Crusaders demurred but many others, whose interest in the Crusade was motivated more by the prospect of plunder than by religious idealism, agreed to the change of plan.

Constantinople was captured and massacre, looting and arson followed. The Venetians occupied themselves with carrying away treasures such as the bronze horses for the portal of the Basilica, the Virgin of Nicopeia and other priceless items which today form part of the Treasury of S. Marco. The epic Crusade is celebrated in a series of paintings in the Doge's Palace in the Sala del Maggior Consiglio.

Constantinople was reconquered in 1261 by the Byzantines but the new Emperor, Michael Paleologus VIII, rather than continue the struggle with the Venetians, allowed them to maintain a colony in Constantinople which in itself was a safeguard against further attack.

During the following century, the Venetians devoted themselves to the struggle against the Genoese and Pisans who were their maritime competitors, as well as against the Saracens who continued to threaten shipping lanes to the Eastern Mediterranean and North Africa.

At home, the Venetians continued to build their island city, setting up trading warehouses and magnificent churches like the Frari and S.S. Giovanni e Paolo (S. Zanipolo). At the same time they confirmed their economic strength by creating the *ducat*, a gold piece which was to become a standard coin in the market places of the world for 500 years.

The commercial success of Venice was not, however, without its problems. One of these problems was the Papacy which expected an obedience in worldly as well as spiritual matters which the Venetians were not prepared to give. One confrontation came to a head at Ferrara, a dukedom of the Ferrara family who were traditionally allies of Venice. Disagreement between the Pope and Venice over a successor to the Marquis Azzo VIII led to a decision by the Pope to excommunicate the Republic and he marshalled his allies in Florence, Pisa and Lombardy against his enemy. This led to the seizure of Venetian goods in Papal territory and caused some dissension within Venice itself where factions headed by the Querini and Tiepolo families set out to overthrow the doge. The street tumult that followed is commemorated in the Merceria behind the Moorish clock tower where you can see a stone carving showing a woman casting a mortar out of the window. The mortar was intended for Bajamonte Tiepolo but missed him and killed one of his supporters.

This rebellion against the authorities led to the creation of one of the most notorious and feared of the Venetian political organizations. This was the Council of Ten, a body set up to maintain law and order which could act quickly in an emergency. The Council could call up armed men and ran its own secret service

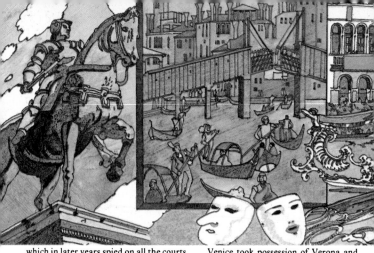

which in later years spied on all the courts and trade centres of Europe bringing back useful information for the Republic.

The power of the Council was demonstrated in 1355 when Doge Marin Falier, irritated by the political impotence of his position and upset by the criticism he received from a group of young aristocrats, tried to kill them at a meeting in the Piazza S. Marco. The plot was discovered, however, and the Council of Ten arrested Falier and his accomplices. They were executed, some by hanging, and the doge died by the executioner's axe. Falier's attempt to overthrow the oligarchal system of government earned him a black banner in the gallery of doge's portraits in the Palazzo Ducale.

Throughout the 14th century the Venetians continued their struggle against their competitors and finally overcame the Genoese fleet at Chióggia. Another enemy, this time on the mainland, was Gian Galeazzo, who led the Viscontis of Milan. He had taken over the cities on the plain of Lombardy and even threatened Florence and other Tuscan cities. Galeazzo was a typical ambitious Lord of the Renaissance and, in the struggle that now took place between him and the Venetians, some of the most famous *condottieri* of Italy took part. Among them were Gattamelata and Colleoni. The equestrian statues of Gattamelata (by Donatello) at Padova and of Colleoni (by Verrochio), near the church of S.S. Giovanni e Paolo in Venice, are regarded as being two of the finest equestrian statues in the world.

Fortunately for Venice, Visconti died of typhoid which also afflicted his soldiers and caused the disintegration of his army. The new feud between the Milanese and the Venetians came to an end.

Venice took possession of Verona and Padua in 1406 and Angelo Correr, who was a high ranking Venetian, became Pope, thus establishing a seal of Papal acceptance for Venice which so often in the past had been at loggerheads with the Pontiff.

Unfortunately this accord did not last long but Venetian diplomacy finally won over its enemies and attempts to deprive the city of its mainland possessions were eventually thwarted.

With Venice now established as a power on land as well as at sea, Venetian pride increased even more and many of the buildings of today were erected showing the wealth and confidence of the Venetian people. This was also a period when some of the interiors of palazzi and churches were embellished with gates and stairways, like those of the Palazzo Ducal, and the walls were covered with paintings by masters such as Gentile Fabbriano, Vivarini, Alemagna and by the Bellini family who, with Carpaccio, left some memorable and detailed paintings of Venetian life in the 15th and early 16th centuries.

The 15th century, though to all intents and purposes the most glorious in Venetian history, was also the one in which the seeds were sown for the Republic's final collapse 300 years later. The Ottoman Turks, to the east, had conquered Byzantium and were spreading westward into the sphere of Venetian and Christian influence. The threat was met by Venice at the battle of Negropont (1416) and finally defeated at Lepanto in 1571. It was one of the most significant victories in maritime history but it left the Republic exhausted. The discovery of America had opened up shipping and trade routes to the east for

the Portugese and this was eventually to have unfortunate effects for Venice. The republic was already beginning to crumble as all highly developed civilizations eventually do but the signs were not apparent as Venice launched itself into its golden age.

During the 15th and 16th centuries the palazzi and the churches continued to rise. Jacopo Sansovino built his beautiful Logetta at the foot of the Campanile and he built the Zecca (Mint) facing the lagoon and the Library of St Mark beside it. In the 16th century, Andrea Palladio arrived with a new range of ideas and built the superb church of S. Giorgio Maggiore and the Redentore on the Giudecca which, today, is the focal point of the celebrations and enormous firework display which takes place at the Feast of the Redentore, the third Sunday in July.

The fever of building and re-building was a symbol of Venetian pride and self-importance and perhaps, too, a form of reassurance for the unvoiced fears that the greatness of Venice was fading. Life became more hectic, carnivals, masques and galas filled the Venetian season and theatre, music and art flourished. Venice became the salon of the whole of cultured Europe but the long decline had begun and the coffers of Venice began to empty. In 1669 Venice lost Crete to the Turks. This was Venice's last overseas possession.

Still the architects of this watery city continued to build. In 1631 Baldassare Longhena began the church of S. Maria della Salute — a building loved by some and hated by others — and in 1668 Andrea Tremignon built S. Moisè, a perfect example of Baroque art with its heavily decorated façade but the spirit of the people had faded and when Napoleon arrived in 1797, the Republic gave up with hardly a sigh.

Now the Serenissima was passed around from hand to hand: from France to the Austrians, then to Italy, then in 1815 back to the Austrians after Napoleon's defeat. In 1849 some of the old spirit revived and Venice shook off the Austrians and set up a government under Doge Daniele Manin but this lasted only until 1866 when the city was finally absorbed by the new United Kingdom of Italy.

This new situation did not, however, put an end to the trials and mixed fortunes which have beset Venice during its long and dramatic history. During the revolution of 1849 bombs were dropped from the air for the first time, from balloons; these were the prelude to a more severe bombardment in World War I when 600 bombs fell on the unfortunate city. Earlier, in 1902, the Campanile had collapsed in the Piazza S. Marco and some may have seen in this catastrophe a portent of evil to come but Venice has survived and an exact replica was erected exactly 1000 years after the first campanile was built.

Now the city is faced with a double threat: corrosion from the acid which floats across from oil refineries and factories in Mestre and Marghera on the mainland and the city also fears the subsidence caused, some believe, by the building of new harbours and the extraction of subterranean gas.

These threats may, in fact, be the final enemy for the Serene Republic. Thus, with a certain bitter irony the most glorious city in the world, a treasure chest of all the best that man is capable of, may disappear due to the same human cupidity and rapaciousness that enabled Venice to become ruler of the Mediterranean.

THE ARTS

A whole book could easily be devoted to the arts in Venice. In fact, many people view the city itself as a spectacular work of art. No visitor should miss the opportunity to enjoy some of the excellent paintings in galleries such as the Accademia (see p. 00). Almost everywhere you go in Venice, you will find an interesting painting, startling architecture or exquisite sculpture. Please see 'Museums and Galleries' (pp. 66–71).

Venice is best known for its excellent artists and, below, we list a short who's who of some of the most celebrated Venetian painters.

Bellini, Jacopo (and sons Gentile and Giovanni): 15th-century artists who had a major impact on the Venetian artistic scene of the time. Giovanni Bellini was particularly well known for the emotion he was able to convey in his paintings. You will find many of his altarpieces, landscapes and Madonnas in Venice.

Canaletto, Antonio (1697–1768): noted for his highly detailed reproductions of 18th-century Venice.

Carpaccio, Vittore (1455–1526): paintings by Carpaccio are very interesting from the historical point of view as they portray Venice in detail in the late 15th and early 16th centuries. He had a strong influence on Canaletto.

Giorgione (*c.* 1478–1510): painted many fine landscapes and was one of the first to marry figures and landscape successfully. Little is known about him but he was probably one of the first to produce small paintings for private houses.

Tiepolo, Giovanni Battista (1696–1770): probably the greatest of the 18th-century Venetians. He decorated several of the most spectacular interiors.

Tintoretto, Jacopo (1518–1594): his best work can be viewed in the cycle of paintings in the Scuola di S. Rocco.

Titian (c. 1490–1576): one of the best places to view works by Titian is in the Frari Church (see p. 00). Many of his works can be found throughout Venice, particularly in the Accademia. He is noted for his vibrant mythological and religious paintings and is regarded as one of the best painters of his time.

Veronese, Paolo (1528–1588): the church of S. Sebastiano was decorated by Veronese. His paintings are usually grand and bright and you can see his well-known *Feast in the House of Levi* in the Accademia (see p. 67).

Tiepolo roundel in the Academy of Arts

PAPERWORK

Passports

All visitors to Italy require a valid passport or, in the case of British subjects, a Visitors Card if you prefer. You may stay for up to three months without a visa if you hold a valid British, Canadian or United States passport. If you plan to remain in Italy for a longer period or if you are visiting for work or study or if you just have some questions about entry to Italy, you should contact your nearest Italian Consulate (please see 'Useful Addresses', p. 29). Citizens of the United Kingdom can apply for a passport at offices in London, Liverpool, Peterborough, Glasgow or Newport in Gwent or enquire at main post offices. Residents in Northern Ireland can apply to the Foreign and Commonwealth Passport Agency, 30 Victoria Street, Belfast. Canadian citizens should apply to the Passport Office, 125 Sussex Drive, Ottawa, Ontario K1A 0G2 or apply in person at offices in Edmonton, Halifax, Montreal, Toronto, Vancouver or Winnipeg. Citizens of the United States can apply to U.S. passport agencies in Boston, Chicago, Miami, New Orleans, New York City, San Francisco or Washington.

You are expected to register with the police within three days of your arrival although your hotel or *pensione* will probably automatically inform them for you.

Insurance

Reciprocal health agreements with Italy entitle **citizens of the United Kingdom** to free medical and dental attention to the standard which Italians normally receive. Before leaving Italy, you should obtain form E111 from the Department of Health and Social Security. If you fall ill in Italy take the form to the local sickness insurance office, known as USL *(Unità Sanitaria Locale)* and you will be given a certificate which entitles you to free treatment from a doctor or a dentist. They will also give you a list of doctors and dentists in the area who are included in the scheme. If you require hospital treatment, the doctor will refer you to a hospital included in the scheme and will issue you with a special certificate. If you have to go into hospital without seeing a doctor, show form E111 to the hospital authorities as soon as you can and ask them to contact the USL. Without the form, you will have to pay for medical treatment at the time and wait for a refund later.

If you would prefer to receive a higher standard of treatment than Italians normally receive, and to ensure speedy treatment, you are advised to take out a separate medical insurance. Private medical schemes give full cover for your visit to Italy. Holiday insurance policies, available from your insurance company or travel agent, often also include insurance against loss of baggage and other risks. **Citizens of the United States and Canada** should ensure that they take out medical insurance to cover them while abroad. Insurance brokers and travel agents can advise and will arrange any additional cover which you require.

If you are **travelling by car** you will require an International Green Card or other insurance for your vehicle.

Currency

The lira (plural lire) is available in the following denominations: coins of 50, 100, 200 and 500 lire and there are notes for 500, 1000, 2000, 5000, 10,000, 20,000, 50,000 and 100,000 lire. Exchange rates fluctuate frequently. You must declare any foreign currency which you bring into Italy and, when you leave, you will only be allowed to take out what you brought in.

There are plenty of banks in Venice (see opening hours p. 26). Thomas Cook has a foreign exchange bureau at the Rialto Bridge and at the Wagons Lits office in the Piazzetta dei Leoncini (sometimes known as Giovanni XXIII) and there are other foreign exchange bureaux around the piazza and along the Calle Larga 22 Marzo. Hotels will also change foreign currency and travellers' cheques but they will not always give you the best rate.

Credit cards are widely accepted, particularly American Express, Diners Club, MasterCard (Eurocard), and Visa. Eurocheques, in lire, are accepted everywhere.

CUSTOMS

Your luggage, passport, currency and hand baggage will be examined when you arrive and again when you leave. If you travel by train, your baggage will be examined on the train.

As well as the duty-free allowances shown in the table below, you may import items for personal use such as clothing, books, some camera equipment, fishing tackle, some film, sports equipment etc. Items of up to 1 million lire can be exported duty-free. Applications to import goods exceeding this amount should be made through a bank or forwarding agent to the customs authorities.

If you take pets into the country, they must be vaccinated against rabies and, for dogs and cats, you will be expected to produce a certificate of Health in English and Italian. Complete information on customs regulations for entering Italy can be obtained from your Italian Consulate.

The chart below summarizes what travellers may bring home duty-free but people under 17 years of age are not entitled to tobacco and drinks allowance. Returning British visitors should remember that no animal may be brought directly into the country. All pets must enter a six month quarantine. No animal is exempt from this, even if already inoculated.

You can take 400,000 lire in or out of Italy at present but these restrictions, like the value of the lira, fluctuate and you should check with Customs and your bank before departure. There are currently no restrictions on other currency but this, too, is subject to change.

Duty-free allowances *subject to change*		Goods bought in a duty-free shop	Goods bought in EEC
Tobacco	Cigarettes or	200	300
Double if you live outside Europe	Cigars *small* or	100	150
	Cigars *large* or	50	75
	Pipe tobacco	250 gm	400 gm
Alcohol	Spirits *over 38.8° proof* or	1 litre	1½ litres
	Fortified or sparkling wine plus	2 litres	3 litres
	Table wine	2 litres	5 litres
Perfume		50 gm	75 gm
Toilet water		250 cc	375 cc
Other goods		£28	£207

US customs permit duty-free $300 retail value of purchases per person, 1 quart of liquor per person over 21, and 100 cigars per person.

GETTING THERE

By Air

From the United Kingdom There are direct scheduled services from London Heathrow each day. These are run by Alitalia and British Airways to Marco Polo airport near Venice. Flights last around two hours. There are charter flights and package tours available. For full up-to-date information on prices and the range of fares available, which include Euro-budget, Pex and Superpex, contact the airline or their appointed travel agents. If you are a student, the Student Travel Bureau at 31 Buckingham Palace Road, London SW1 (tel: 01-828 2082) should be able to give you advice. There are charter flights and package tours available.

From Canada There are direct services from Toronto and Montreal by Alitalia and CP Air. The address of Alitalia is 120 Adelaide St West, Suite 1202, Ontario N5H 2EI (tel: 363 1348). Fare conditions are the same as for those flying from the United States.

From the United States There are services to Venice, usually via Milan, from New York City and Boston run by TWA and Alitalia. The address of Alitalia is 666 5th Avenue, New York City, New York 101103 (tel: 212 903 3300). There are also services run by Pan Am from New York City. Fares vary according to the time of year and type of flight etc. The cheapest are APEX and Budget, both of which must be booked in advance. For full up-to-date details, you should contact the airlines.

When you arrive in Italy, you can travel to Venice (Piazzale Roma) by coach from the Marco Polo airport at the northeast end of the lagoon. Alternatively, you can travel by vaporetto steamer to Piazza S. Marco. There is also a motorboat taxi service which takes four people. Always make sure that you agree on the fares before boarding. The taxi will drop you at your hotel or at the nearest landing point.

By Rail
From the United Kingdom There are direct services from London (Victoria) via Dover/Boulogne and Milan. The journey lasts about 25 hours but you can take a break from your travels for a while if you wish and join another train later. You can book your seat with British Rail. If you are under 26, ask for details of young person's passes and special fares. Details of motorail services are available from British Rail. The Italian State Tourist Office should also be able to help you. (See 'Useful Addresses' p. 29.)

If you want to travel in luxury accommodation, the Venice Simplon Orient Express runs as a first-class only train from Victoria Station in London to Venice via Paris and Milan. If you live in the United States or Canada, you should contact the Orient Express representative at 115 Avenue of the Americas, New York City, New York 10036 (tel: 212 302 5066).

From the United States and Canada You can purchase special tickets for unlimited travel anywhere in Western Europe except Great Britain and you should buy these before you leave home. Your nearest Italian State Tourist Office should be able to offer advice (see 'Useful Addresses' p. 29).

By Car
There are car ferries from Britain to the Continent. You can leave Dover for Boulogne or Ostend, travelling with Townsend Thoreson or, travelling with Sealink, you can leave from Dover or Folkestone for Calais or Boulogne. The Sally Line will take you from Ramsgate to Dunkerque. The journey to France by ferry usually takes around two hours. Hoverspeed operates from Dover to Calais or Boulogne and the journey takes about 35–45 minutes. Ask the ferry operators for up-to-date information on frequency of crossings and for details of any other possible crossing points which interest you. There are good roads to Venice all the way from the Channel ports.

By Bus/Coach
From the United Kingdom There are regular coach services from London (Victoria Coach Station) via Milan. Ask for details from the Victoria Coach Station or from the Student Travel Bureau, 31 Buckingham Palace Road, London SW1.

Euroways runs a luxury coach service to Venice in the summer months via Paris and Milan. For information, contact Euroways Express Coaches/Wallace Arnold, 52 Grosvenor Gardens, London W1.

Travelling to your hotel
If you make the last part of your trip by steamer you will probably require a porter at the Piazza S. Marco landing stage. Porters *(Portabagaglio* or *facchino)* run services to different areas of Venice and carry luggage from baggage stations *(stazione bagaglio)* on a hand cart. There is a fixed fee laid down by the Tourist authority. If you want to book a porter from the airport, ring Stazione portabagaglio, S. Marco 32385 or 700545 or ask someone at the Information stand to do it for you.

GETTING YOUR BEARINGS

Unlike most cities, Venice is small and compact enough to be explored in its entirety in just one or two weeks, although many people never stray from the tourist tracks to the main monuments. To make the most of Venice, first get a mental picture of the shape of the islands which make up the city and its various areas or *sestieres.*

There are six *sestieri* — three on each side of the Canal Grande which snakes like a reversed 'S' through Venice. On the west side Dorsoduro stretches from the docks (Stazione Marittime) to the Dogana (Customs House) and the church of S. Maria della Salute. S. Polo and S. Croce are also on the west side. They are tucked into the bend of the canal between the Rio Nuovo in front of the railway station and the Rialto Bridge. On the east side, S. Marco is in the lower bend of the Canal, Cannaregio stretches northwest towards the railway station and Castello stretches westward to the claw-like end of the island past the Arsenale.

The most well-trodden path through Venice runs from the railway station to Piazza S. Marco and from the Piazza over the Accademia bridge through S. Polo and S. Croce back across the Scalzi bridge to the railway station. There are plenty of signs along this route indicating either Ferrovia (railway station), Piazzale Roma or Piazza S. Marco according to the direction in which you are travelling.

It is more fun to wander off at random down any little street that takes your fancy and if you memorize each campanile as you pass, you will seldom get lost as each tower is very distinctive and you can usually spot them up narrow canals or streets or over the roof tops of Piazzas. They are, in fact, 'lighthouses' for the more adventurous visitor to Venice.

Few of the streets of Venice are as straight as they appear on a map which is why people find it strange that Venetians often tell you to go *sempre diritto* (straight ahead) when you ask the way. But don't worry about it: sooner or later you will come to a well known place and you can take your bearings again.

If there is a specific house that you want to find then you may have a real problem as Venetian houses are numbered irrespective of streets and are counted from one to whatever the number of the last house in a particular *sestiere* may be. The only answer to this problem is to ask Vene-

Some Campani

San Bartolomeo

San Marco

San Giorgio Maggiore

San Moisè

tians in the area, particularly people who normally make deliveries, such as the postman. Most Venetians are very helpful if you ask them.

Apart from getting your bearings on Venice itself, all you need is to have a clear picture of the other islands of the lagoon. Giudecca lies to the south across the Giudecca canal from Dorsoduro and the Lido lies further out forming a sandy barrier against the Adriatic. To the north of the lagoon lie S. Michele, which is the ceme-tery island; Murano where the glassworks are; Burano home of the lacemakers and a good place for Sunday lunch; Torcello, one of the first inhabited islands and with an interesting church. To the south, the lagoon is fairly empty except for a few islands in the area near Venice which were once occupied by monasteries and hospitals but they are now slowly being abandoned. At the southern end of the lagoon you will find the fishing village of Chióggia.

f Venice

San Giorgio dei Greci

Santa Maria Formosa

Santi Apostoli

San Zaccaria

GETTING AROUND

There are four ways of getting around in Venice: by gondola, motorboat, waterbus and on foot. By far the most desirable is the gondola.

Gondolas

The strange looking craft called the gondola is the most ancient form of Venetian transport and, in the past, all patrician families had their own gondola, much in the same way as the squirearchy had their own carriages. The boat is flat bottomed and has the ability to turn in its own length. All gondolas are painted black by tradition. In 1562 it was decreed that all gondolas should be black in order to prevent ostentation by leading families. For decoration, only two brass sea-horses were permitted and the *ferro* — a blade which is still used on the prow. Each of the six sections on the blade is said to represent one of the six *sestieri* into which Venice is divided.

Gondolas are propelled by gondoliers who are skilled at manoeuvering their long craft around the blind corners of small canals and uttering special cries that warn unseen oncoming traffic of their approach. Traditionally, gondoliers also sing romantic songs but we have rarely heard any of them do it well. Most are rather taciturn unless they hope to earn an extra tip by acting as a guide as well as helmsman.

The cost of hiring a gondola is considerable but the pleasure derived from a gondola ride far outweighs the price. A cheap way of making a gondola journey is to join one of the tourist flotillas which are offered by travel agents. These usually include a singer and accordion or guitar player.

If you take a gondola ride, either on your own or with a small party, check the price against the rate laid down by the authorities. If you enjoy bargaining you can sometimes get a better round-trip price.

In addition to paying the gondolier, save a few lire for the *ganzer* (hookman). He holds the gondola against the quayside with a hook and helps you in and out of the craft — a very useful service.

Water Taxis

Water taxis are luxurious motorboats with polished wooden hulls and cabins and they are the quickest way of getting around Venice. They are also fairly expensive and there is an hourly tariff within Venice but it is wise to negotiate a price before departure. The charge is usually for the whole boat which seats up to four people comfortably.

Vaporetti

Water buses are called *vaporetti*. Sometimes, on the fast runs they are called *motoscafi* and on the longer runs, *motonave*. The steamers are run on diesel and the Canal Grande is usually full of shouts and confusion as they come alongside the floating barges from which you embark and disembark. They are not the most comfortable method of transport but they are cheap and, by travelling on them, you participate in the hustle and bustle of Venetian life.

There are 25 services run by the *Azienda Consorzio Transporti Veneziano* (ACTV) whose headquarters are at Campo dell Alberno, by S. Angelo on the Canal Grande. Here you can obtain timetables and other information. *Diretto* or *direttissimo* services are the quickest and most expensive and those called *accelerato* (Venetians sometimes just call them *vaporetto*) are the slowest despite their name. The *accelerato* allows you to see more of the city as you pass. There is often a difference in price betweeen the services and an *accelerato* ticket will not allow you on to a *diretto*. *Circolare* make a round trip. Services are shown on the maps on pp. 33-63. Here is a list of the services you are most likely to use.

1. *Accelerato* between the railway station or Piazzale Roma and the Lido via Piazza S. Marco.
2. *Diretto* leaves the Piazzale Roma via the Rio Nuovo and joins route no. 1 in the Canal Grande. It then carries on past the Piazza S. Marco and S. Zaccaria to the Lido.
3. *Direttissimo* (summer only) a non-stop service from the car park to the Piazza S. Marco.
4. *Touristico* (summer only) from the Piazzale Roma along the Canal Grande, via the Piazza S. Marco to the Lido. The *Touristico* makes fewer stops than on the accelerato route no. 1.
5. *Circolare*. This route is split into two circular services covering the right and the left of the city.
6. *Motonave* travels between the Riva degli Schiavoni and the Lido.
12. *Motonave* to Burano and Torcello from Fondamenta Nuove near the Gesuiti.

18. *Servizio touristico balneare* (summer only) runs to Murano and the Lido from Fondamenta Nuove near the Gesuiti.

On foot

Specific walks are suggested on pp. 72-93. Even with the aid of a map, Venice is an easy city in which to get lost. Streets are narrow and never seem to lead out where you expect. Don't worry. The city is so small that, in whichever direction you decide to stroll, you are bound to come across a familiar street or landmark. Most Venetians are very helpful if you ask for directions. Do not be worried by narrow, shadowy streets which can sometimes look sinister. Venice has the lowest crime rate in Italy, probably because it is so densely populated that you are always within call of someone and, being an island, it offers limited means of escape to muggers and other miscreants.

The one problem when walking around Venice is getting across the Canal Grande. If you do not always want to have to walk back to one of the three bridges, Ponte degli Scalzi, the Ponte di Rialto or the Ponte dell'Accademia, try to locate the cross canal ferry services, known as *traghetti*, before you set off. These ferries are flat bottomed gondola punts on which you stand as you are rowed across. There is a modest fee.

Ferries usually operate from early working hours until later in the evening. Main ferry crossings run to and from the following stops:

S. Maria del Giglio (Zobenigo) to the Salute
S. Samuele to S. Barnaba (near Ca' Rezzonico)
S. Angelo to S. Tomà
Riva del Carbon to Riva del Vin
Ca' d'Oro to Rialto markets
S. Marcuola to the Fondaco dei Turchi

ACCOMMODATION

Although Venice is renowned for its great hotels, most of the accommodation available is much less luxurious and, if you like an authentic local flavour, these less luxurious hotels can be more fun. Most of the hotels are in the S. Marco and Castello *sestieri*, (areas) where costs are quite high but there is accommodation all over Venice if you don't mind being away from the vicinity of the Piazza S. Marco.

Many of the hotels are in old palazzi which have been modernized. There is often a wide range of room sizes available and it is best to inspect the room before accepting it.

There are four categories of hotel accommodation and three categories of *pensioni* and *locande* (inns). The least expensive accommodation is often in a rooming house, sometimes calling itself a hotel, which does not provide service or food.

As with everywhere in Italy, prices are fixed by the Ministry of Tourism according to the facilities offered. These prices are shown in a list in the hotel reception and also in your room. Extra taxes, according to the category of your hotel, are tourist tax at roughly 17% and IVA (Value Added Tax) at 10–18%. These extra costs are often included in the quoted price and service charges are automatically included.

Venice has an excellent hotel reservation service at the railway station and Piazzale Roma garage but it is better to reserve your room ahead — Venice does not really have an off-season except in mid-winter when many of the hotels are closed. If you are staying in a hotel, you are required by law to obtain an official receipt.

Youth Hostels: a complete list of accommodation is published annually and is available at Italian State Tourist Offices (see 'Useful Addresses' p. 29). It is best to make your reservation in advance.

Camping: there is no camping in Venice itself but there is a site at Mestre. You can obtain a list of camping sites from the Venice Tourist Office (see p. 29).

Hotels: the following list of hotels is divided into the six *sestieri* of Venice (see p. 13). We have selected a number of hotels which appealed to us and graded them, relatively speaking, as expensive, moderately priced and inexpensive.

S. Marco

Bauer Grünwald Hotel, Campo S. Moisè (tel: 707022), overlooks the Canal Grande. It is spacious, efficient and every-thing a grand hotel should be apart from the poor taste façade. Expensive.

Bonvecchiati, Calle Goldoni (tel: 850171). This hotel has a pleasant atmosphere, it provides good service and is decorated with the owner's collection of 20th-century paintings. Expensive.

La Fenice e des Artistes, Campiello della Fenice (tel: 32333). Here, you will be given friendly service in a pleasant atmosphere. Another advantage of this hotel is its proximity to the theatre. Moderately priced.

Torino, Calle delle Ostreghe (tel: 70522), near S. Maria del Giglio. This is an attractive little hotel with a small, luxuriant garden. Moderately priced.

Do Pozzi off Calle Larga 22 Marzo (tel: 707855). A pleasant little hotel with a small garden. Inexpensive.

Castello

Danieli, Riva degli Schiavoni (tel: 26480). Like all hotels on the Riva, there is a good view of lagoon. Chopin stayed in the romantic old part of the hotel. The service here is slightly impersonal. Expensive.

Gabrielli Sandwirth, Riva degli Schiavoni (tel: 31580). This stylish but friendly Gothic palazzo has a modernised interior and gardens. Expensive.

Londra Palace, Riva degli Schiavoni (tel: 700533). This is a grand, comfortable hotel. Tchaikovsky wrote his fourth symphony here. Expensive.

Paganelli, Riva degli Schiavoni (tel: 24324). An unpretentious, well looked after hotel in a good position. Moderately priced.

Savoia e Jolanda, Riva degli Schiavoni (tel: 706644). A friendly family hotel. Moderately priced.

La Residenza, Campo Bandiera e Moro (tel: 85315). Could do with some renovation but this is an atmospheric Gothic palazzo without pretentions. Inexpensive.

Scandinavia, Campo S. Maria Formosa (tel: 705965). A well-kept, clean, modern hotel. Inexpensive.

Dorsoduro and Giudecca

Cipriani, Giudecca (tel: 707744). Spacious gardens with a swimming pool, tennis court and good food. This hotel is really what you might expect from the man who owns the Orient Express. Expensive.

Accademia, near Accademia (tel: 704733). This *pensione* is in a lovely old 17th-century palazzo with gardens. Moderately priced.

American, near Campo S. Vito (tel: 704733). Bright, newly furnished hotel for those who prefer pleasant efficiency to atmosphere. Moderately priced.

Montin, Rio delle Eremite, Fondamenta di Borgo (tel: 23307). This modest *locanda* (inn) near S. Trovaso has a super garden restaurant. Inexpensive.

Seguso, Fondamenta Zattere dei Gesuati (tel: 22340). An unpretentious family *pensione* with a friendly Anglophile proprietor and a good view across to Giudecca. Inexpensive.

Cannaregio and S. Croce

S. Cassiano, Calle della Rosa, S. Croce (tel: 705477). Overlooks the Canal Grande opposite Ca'd'Oro. A pleasant old refurbished palazzo with a grand atmosphere. Moderately priced.

Madonna dell'Orto. Fondamenta Madonna dell'Orto (tel: 700555). A charming refurbished old palazzo with large rooms but it is some way to the Piazza S. Marco. Moderately priced.

Giorgione, near the Campo S.S. Apostoli, Cannaregio (tel: 25810). A tranquil hotel with large rooms. Inexpensive.

At the railway station and near Calle dell'Ascensione, you can rest at one of Venice's 'day hotels' *(albergo diurno)*. There are several amenities but, as the name suggests, there is no accommodation for sleeping.

The Gritti Palace Hotel

FOOD AND DRINK

Venice is not known as a great gourmet city but most of the restaurants serve appetising, if limited, menus in which pasta and fish dishes play a large role. There are some exceptions where meals are as good as anywhere in Europe but the bill you are given will also be as high. On the other hand, you can have an agreeable meal at a *trattoria* with a pleasant ambience for a much more modest price.

Many guide books suggest that it is good for the budget to make do with a snack at midday and have a full meal in the evening. The snag with this arrangement is that Venetian life is geared to a total shutdown in the middle of the day to allow time for lunch and it is therefore difficult to fill the hours around midday usefully.

Lunch in a tranquil *trattoria* can make an enjoyable break in the day's sightseeing, especially if you choose one with a garden. You need not eat expensively —

pasta and salad with fruit to follow is often quite adequate with a little wine. Alternatively, you can buy sandwiches or take-away snacks and have a picnic at the *Parco della Rimembranze* in the S. Elena area or across at the Lido.

The Venetian menu is not extensive although, in the more expensive restaurants, they will serve up standard dishes in a stylish and original way. You could start with *prosciutto e melone* (Parma ham and melon), *pasta e fagioli* (pasta and beans) or a typically Venetian version of this called *risi e bisi*. Alternatively, you could try shellfish which are always fresh. Hungry Italians sometimes fit in some kind of pasta between the starter and the main dish. The main course often consists either of some form of veal or chicken. *Fegato alla Veneziana* (liver and onions) is expensive but fresh and delicious. Fish is a popular food in Venice as you might expect. Some of the fish you will find on your menus include *aragosta* (lobster), *calamari* (squid), *granzeola* (crab), *lupo di mare* (bass), *rombo* (turbot), *polpetto* (young octopus), *sogliola* (sole), *San Pietro* (John Dory), *triglia* (red mullet), *sarda* (sardine).

Other terms which you might find useful when dining out include the following:

bread	*pane*
butter	*burro*
coffee	*caffè*
entrèes	*pietanze*
fish	*pesce*
fruit	*frutta*
Hors d'oeuvre	*antipasto*
menu	*un menù*
mineral water	*acqua minerale*
milk	*latte*
pepper	*pepe*
salt	*sale*
soup	*minestra*
sugar	*zucchero*
dessert	*un dessert*
tea	*un tè*
vegetables	*contorno*

For information on widely consumed non-alcoholic beverages, please see p. 26.

White wine *(vino bianco)* and red wine *(vino rosso)* are available in most restaurants but many Venetians prefer just to ask for the house wine *(vino della casa)* as this is usually of a good standard and fairly inexpensive. Local wines are pleasant but they are not outstanding.

Venetians like to take their time over meals and it's best to allow two hours for lunch and more for the evening meal which usually begins between 1900 and 2130 although a few restaurants take last orders later. A service charge of 15% is usually included in your bill but, in the more expensive restaurants, you may leave a little extra for personal attention.

The following list of restaurants will help you to find an enjoyable meal in the top, medium and inexpensive categories of establishment but there are many more which you will soon discover for yourself. We have included the ones we know but not the large 'typical' ones which are usually patronized almost entirely by tourists.

S. Marco

This is the best hunting ground for restaurants, especially between the Piazza S. Marco and the Rialto bridge.

Antico Martini, Campo S. Fantin (tel: 24121). Famous traditional restaurant with an extensive menu, patronized by company executives and fashionable people. There is also a nightclub here. Expensive.

La Caravella restaurant in the **Saturnia e International Hotel**, Calle Larga XXII Marzo (tel: 70891). A grand style restaurant for tourists with money to spare. The food is up to standard and the service is efficient although you may feel overwhelmed by it. The hotel also runs the **El Cortile** restaurant in a patio at the back which is less grand but charming and ideal for a summer lunch. Expensive.

Harry's Bar, Calle Vallaresso (tel: 85331/36797). The Hemingway cliché restaurant patronized by people from the United States and those who appreciate good food. Expensive.

Noemi, Calle dei Fabbri (tel: 25238). Low key elegance is the style of this restaurant which serves delicious and well presented food that sophisticated palates will appreciate. Expensive.

La Colomba, Frezzeria (tel: 21175). A large, often crowded, typically Venetian restaurant where excellent 20th-century paintings hang. There is a terrace in the calle. Moderately priced.

Al Teatro, Campo S. Fantin (tel: 21052). Lively restaurant, bar and pizzeria (in separate areas). You will be served with good food and there is plenty going on to make an enjoyable evening. Moderate.

Antica Carbonara, Calle le Bembo, near the Rialto (tel: 25479). Small old world restaurant with Risorgimento decor. The menu is unambitious but the food is enjoyable. Inexpensive.

Stagneri, Calle Stagneri (tel: 27341). Small friendly place run by a patrona who keeps an eye on you, the food and hopeful customers at the door. Good home cooking and good atmosphere. Inexpensive.

Castello

Arcimboldo, Rielo dei Furlani, near S. Zaccaria (tel: 86569). Unlike most Venetian restaurants, this one does not go

The baker takes a break

in for fish but specializes in interesting combinations of veal, chicken, fruit and vegetables. Moderately priced.

Corte Sconta, Calle del Pestrin — round the corner to the east of Campo Bandiera e Moro (tel: 27024). A small fish restaurant, serving excellent and imaginative fish dishes. Moderately priced.

Giardinetto di Severino, Salizzada Zorzi, near S. Maria Formosa (tel: 85332). Appetising traditional dishes are served here in high vaulted rooms with a brick fireplace or under an awning in the garden. Moderately priced.

Cannaregio
Al Paradiso Perduto, Fondamenta Misericordia (tel: 21457). Many young people find their way to the long, dark interior of this 'lost paradise' which stays open late and serves traditional pasta and risotto dishes. Inexpensive.

Antico Molo, Fondamenta degli Ormesini (no telephone). Very small, simple *trattoria* on the Rio della Misericordia. Excellent risottos, pastas and traditional dishes are served here. Inexpensive.

Roma, Fondamenta Scalzi. A large, popular restaurant attached to a hotel near the railway station with a terrace restaurant on the Canal Grande. The food is simple and satisfying and the view of the canal is absorbing. Inexpensive.

Rialto to Dorsoduro
La Furatola, Calle Lunga S. Barnaba (tel: 708594). A small, inconspicuous restaurant near Campo S. Barnaba which provides a pleasant, tranquil haven and good, fresh fish. Moderately priced.

Alla Madonna, Calle della Madonna, near the Rialto (tel: 23824). A popular fish restaurant, crowded with families on Sundays and, on weekdays, it is full of tourists. Good abundant food. Moderately priced.

Montin, Fondamenta di Borgo, near S. Trovaso (tel: 23307). Interesting paintings hang in the rooms and there is a walled garden with tables under a pergola. Your appetite will be satisfied by delicious, uncomplicated, well served food. Moderately priced.

S. Croce and S. Polo
Da Fiore, Calle dei Scalater, near Campo S. Polo (tel: 37208). Fresh fish and shellfish are the main dishes in this popular local restaurant. Moderately priced.

Antica Bassetta, Salizzada Zusto, near S. Giacomo dell' Orio (tel: 37687). A simple *trattoria* off the beaten track with home-cooked pasta and risottos. Inexpensive.

Pordenone, Calle Madonetta (tel: 89482). A small friendly trattoria serving traditional dishes. Inexpensive.

Burano
The island of Burano teems with restaurants along its main street, Via B. Galuppi. The most famous, and the most fun, is **Tre Stelle da Romano,** an old artist and fisherman's haunt with a lively and noisy atmosphere. Large Italian family parties dine here. It's best to reserve a table in advance at weekends (tel: 730030).

Chióggia
The restaurants on Il Corso get their fish straight from the boats in the harbour. They are **El Gato, Bella Venezia** and **La Mano Amica.**

Lido
The Lido has several good restaurants of the kind found in seaside resort areas. For a place with local atmosphere, go to the port of Malamocco where you can dine at **Al Porticciolo da Danilo** by the harbour (tel: 768384).

Murano
If you go to Murano to visit the glass factories and want to stop for a meal, try **Ai Frati,** a simple but pleasant fish restaurant (tel: 736694).

Torcello
The **Locanda Cipriani** (owned by Harry's Bar) provides rural simplicity and very good food in another of Hemingway's haunts.

Cafés and Bars
If you want a quick snack or an aperitif in an interesting place try one of the following cafés or bars.

Bar Ducale, Calle delle Ostreghe, near Sta Maria del Giglio in S. Marco (tel: 710002). A small bar with good staff who know how to mix drinks well and make appetizing sandwiches.

Florians, Piazza S. Marco (tel: 85338). A most romantic and plush café with mirrors. Former patrons include Chopin and Wagner. You pay for the privilege but it is worth it.

Quadri, Piazza S. Marco (tel: 22105). This is always a crowded café, especially for morning coffee as it catches the morning sun. An orchestra plays nostalgic tunes but the prices remind you that all nations belong to the brotherhood of inflation!

Harry's Bar, Calle Vallaresso (tel: 85331). Where would Hemingway have been without Harry's and Harry's without Hemingway? It doesn't matter as the drinks are good and the sandwiches excellent in this smartly run bar.

Paolin, Campo S. Stefano, also known as Campo Francesco Morosini (tel: 25576). Take the kids to Paolin for great ice cream and soft drinks. Adults are well served here too.

SHOPPING

Some of the smartest and most expensive shops in Italy operate from tiny premises in the *sestiere* S. Marco, mainly in the Piazza, the Calle Larga XXII Marzo and along the Merceria and surrounding streets. Less expensive, but equally interesting shops and craft studios can be found in Dorsoduro on the route between the Rialto and the Accademia bridge.

The following is a list of some of the shops which have appealed to us but there are many others which may interest you.

S. Marco

This is the area for smart clothes, the best glass, books (antiquarian and modern) and for hairdressers and beauty salons. Calle Larga 22 Marzo, being near the de luxe hotels, naturally has some of the smartest women's clothes shops. For high fashion look in **Fendi** and **Valentino** and, at nearby Frezzeria, in **La Coupole**. Near the Fenice, in Campo S. Fantin have a look in **Elisabetta alla Fenice** and the **Rosella Boutique** at Calle del Teatro.

Along the Merceria there are many good shops with attractive windows. At the upper end of the price range, shops include **Gucci** and the **Corner Shop**, which specialize in sports wear, and the **Duca d'Aosta** shops with their men's and women's sections, selling stylish well-made clothes. Another expensive shop which goes in for traditional styles is **Elite** in Calle Larga S. Marco. For specially-made men's shirts and women's blouses go to **Camiceria S. Marco** in Calle Vallaresso.

You will also find well-made Italian leather shops in this street at the **Bottega Veneta** and at **Vogini** in Calle Larga Ascensione on the way to Piazza S. Marco. Less expensive stylish shoes can be found at **Zecchi** in the Merceria but if you are looking for designer shoes and bags you should go to **Elysée** in Calle Goldoni. There are many leather specialists along the Merceria and **La Paragina's** selection is very good.

Venetian glass is available everywhere in Venice, although some of it is of a low quality that the glassmakers of Murano still turn out some exquisite work. You can see artistic examples of glassware in the museum at Murano or in the Murano factory showrooms of **Barovier e Toso** and **Nason e Moretti** on the Fondamenta Vetrai or at **Vivarini's** in Fondamenta Serenella.

In Venice itself, some very fine glasswork can be found at **Venini** in the Piazzetta Leoncini. There are, of course, showrooms where every conceivable type of glassware from miniature penguins to spouting fountains are exhibited to satisfy every taste. **Canedese** and **Pauly** in Piazza S. Marco both have a very comprehensive stock and **Salviati** also has a factory on the Canal Grande.

The manufacture of books was a major industry in Venice when the Republic was at its height and the art of bookbinding, as well as the early skills of printing and marbling of end papers, still survive. One of the best shops specializing in marbled papers and handbound volumes *etc* is **Paolo Olbi** in the Calle della Mandola. **Studio Bibliografico 'la Fenice'** in Calle del Fruttarol sells interesting antiquarian books. If you fancy a reprint of an old book or map, then visit the **Libreria Editrice Filippi** in Calle Bissa, off Campo S. Bartolommeo or their branch in Calle Paradiso which is across the Ponte di Rialto. If you are looking for a big bookshop with a good selection of books, including English and American texts, try **Fantoni's** on Salizzada S. Luca or **Bertoni** who has a good stock of second hand books at his shop in Calle Mandola, near Campo S. Angelo. They both have good selections of books on art and architecture.

Lace is still made in Burano although much of the lace in Venetian shops probably comes from the Far East. A few shops still sell genuine Venetian lace. Among them is the **Jesurum** on the little Fondamenta by the Ponte Canonica, behind the Basilica. You will also find household linen and blouses *etc* trimmed with lace at **Martinuzzi** in the Piazza S. Marco.

Other shops in the S. Marco *sestiere* which are a little unusual include **Il Prato** at Frezzeria, where you will find imaginatively painted masks and other ingenious bric-a-brac and the **Legatoria Piazzese** which has a surprising collection of papers printed from old blocks. In the food line, there is a delicious bread and pastry shop called **Il Fornaio** where bread is sculpted into amusing Baroque figures, sheaves of corn *etc*.

Rialto to Dorsoduro

Over the Ponte di Rialto, several shops sell good value leather goods, jewellery, belts and linen. There is a market here and little shops which stand discreetly behind the market stalls. Among these is **Canale**, in the Ruga Rialto, which specializes in colourful ceramic jewellery and belts. **Paolo Baruffaldi** sells prints and masks.

You will find many little craft studios in the small streets on the way from the Rialto to the Accademia, most of them run by the craftsman who does the work. **Signor Blum** at Calle Lunga, S. Barnaba makes beautiful modern pictures in coloured woods and, at **Lascialuppa**, another craftsman works in wood making, among other things, exquisite models of gondolas.

Cannaregio

Generally speaking, the shops of Cannaregio cater for the Venetian working people rather than tourists but near the Rialto end there is a very smart women's fashion shop.

This is called **Coin** on the Ponte de l'Ogio, close to Campo S. Bartolommeo and it is housed in a fine Gothic palazzo.

If you feel like being a little more extravagant and would like to buy some real antique stonework then you should find out when the auction is next on at the **Palazzo Giovanelli** on the Strada Nova. Statues and fragments of buildings are always on show here and you can find out when the next sale takes place either at the palazzo or at the Tourist Office.

ENTERTAINMENT

Throughout the 18th and 19th century Venice devoted much of its energy to carnivals, theatre, concerts and all kinds of festivities. The tradition continues today with annual festivals and regular special events (see pp. 30−31), theatre, opera seasons and art exhibitions. Unlike many large cities, however, Venice does not offer much in the way of night clubs and floorshows. Perhaps this is because Venice itself is the best show of all, especially in summer when the Piazza S. Marco is full of Venetians, visitors, the sound of music and the murmur of conversation. The buildings loom as pale and mysterious as stage scenery before which actors from all over the world perform their parts.

Most theatres are not open all year but, to check which events are going on during your stay, see the local publication, *Ospite di Venezia* which is free or consult the local newspaper *Il Gazzettino*.

Theatre

La Fenice, Campo S. Fantin, S. Marco (tel: 710161 or 710336). This elegant 18th-century opera house has a sumptuous interior decorated with painted panels, gilt and plaster work and it seats 1500 people. Concerts, ballet and opera are performed here and the elegantly decorated adjoining rooms are used for festivals and special events. The theatre can be visited outside rehearsal hours but it is usually closed in August.

Teatro Goldoni, Calle Goldoni, S. Marco (tel: 705422). This 18th-century theatre was built by the Vendramin family and named after the famous Venetian dramatist, Carlo Goldoni. Plays are usually shown here.

Teatro Malibran, S. Giovanni Grisostomo, S. Polo. The theatre was built in the late 17th century by the Grimani family. This theatre puts on mainly ballet, concerts and opera.

Theatres which are used occasionally include Teatro del Ridotto, Calle Valla-

resso (5222939); and Teatro a l'Avogaria, Calle de l'Avogari (706130).

Cinemas

Most films are in Italian or dubbed. Ask at the Tourist Office for daily information. The main cinemas are: Accademia, Dorsoduro (5260188); Olimpia, S. Marco (705439); Palazzo del Cinema, Lido (5260188); Ritz, S. Marco (704429); Rossini, S. Marco (5230322); Centrale, S. Marco (28201).

Nightclubs and Casino

Nightclubbing is not a popular Venetian pastime but Venice caters for visitors who enjoy dancing or gambling and the following places are certainly worth a visit.

Casino Municipale, Lungomare G. Marconi, Lido (tel: 5260626 or 5260696). Open from 1500−0300. The Lido Casino has roulette, blackjack, trente et quarante *etc.* This is one of the most famous casinos in the world and there is a restaurant and a nightclub. Open April−September.

Casino Municipale, Palazzo Vendramin-Calergi, Strada Nuova, Cannaregio. You can also make a grand entry from the Canal Grande (tel: 710211). This is the Venetian half of the Lido Casino and offers similar facilities including the Casanova nightclub. Open October−March. Hours 1500−0300.

Martini Nightclub, Campo S. Fantin, near the Fenice theatre (tel: 24121 or 37027). Open 2200−0330. The usual cosmopolitan atmosphere reigns here at the main centre of Venetian nightlife.

You might also care to visit **El Souk** near the Accademia (tel: 700731) which is open every evening except Wednesdays from 2130−0200. The big hotels also have occasional dancing and there are piano bars at the Londra Hotel and Lucien's restaurant on the Riva degli Schiavoni. Similar facilities are also available at the Monaco e Canal Grande hotel in Calle Vallaresso and at Cipriani's on Giudecca.

The interior of Teatro La Fenice

SPORTS & ACTIVITIES

Venice is not really suitable for most sporting activities other than jogging as there is not much room for sports grounds but children often use some of the campos for roller skating or bicycle riding.

There are, however, rowing clubs which you can join if you can swim. These provide you with the opportunity to enjoy the unusual and sometimes hazardous pleasure of propelling yourself around the Venetian canals in a skiff. For information, contact Societa Cannottieri Francesco Querini, Fondamenta Nuove (tel: 5222039) or the Societa Cannottieri 'Diadora' on the Lido (tel: 765742).

On the Lido the range of activities is far greater than in Venice itself.

Cycling Giorgio Barbieri at 5 Via Zara on the Lido rents out bicycles for easy rides along the flat roads of the Lido.

Flying You may feel it is worthwhile to take a flight over the lagoon — a splendid experience which brings into focus the extraordinary environment which created the Venetian Republic. Contact Aeroclub di Venezia, Lido Airport (760808).

Golf The flat sandy Lido provides excellent terrain for an 18-hole course at the Alberoni Club at the southern end of the island (tel: 831015).

Horse Riding At Ca'Bianca you can hire a horse for a ride along the sand. Lessons are also given here (tel: 5265162).

Sailing The Excelsior sailing club at Lungomare G. Marconi is run by the Excelsior hotel and rents out small craft.

Sauna The sports centre Lido at Lungomare G. Marconi has a sauna and a gymnasium (tel: 5268797).

Tennis The Lido tennis club is at Via S. Gallo (tel: 5260054) and the Tennis Union Club is in Via Fausta (tel: 968134). Sporting club Venezia at Via Parri has 10 courts, three of which are covered and a swimming pool in which you can relax after a hard game (tel: 770722).

CHILDREN'S VENICE

Visiting Venice if you have children with you is probably best achieved by living outside the city at nearby resorts like Lido di Jesolo and making trips to the island on alternate days. If this is not possible try to find a hotel or *pensione* that has a garden because children often find urban Venice trying. As children have a very limited interest in buildings and works of art, we must devise ways of keeping them amused. Here are a few suggestions:

1. Take them about on vaporetti as much as possible. The occasional gondola ride also does much for flagging spirits.
2. Make long refreshment stops at the campos as you pass by on your walks.
3. Play games of I spy or spot the animals in paintings.
4. Get to know the ice cream shops and toy shops. Children develop a sense of location amazingly quickly when they know of these landmarks.

The best areas for visiting a café in the Piazza S. Marco are Riva degli Schiavone or by the Rialto. A popular place for ice cream is Paolin in Campo S. Stefano but there are plenty of others.

There are several toy shops, including a very good two-floor shop in Campo Manin, and children will immediately realise that the statue of Manin with a winged lion in the centre of the campo is useful for climbing on.

Glass factories are good for at least an hour's entertainment and if you take the children to the glass museum they can spot the styles of glassware in the shops later.

There are two public parks in which children can run around — the Giardini Pubblici at the eastern end of the Riva degli Schiavone and the Giardini Papadopoli near Piazzale Roma. This park is smaller but worth a visit if you're in the area. Of course, the best open space is on the Lido and lunch hours spent there help to make a good long break in the day.

GENERAL INFORMATION

Animals In Venice, the most common animal is the cat. You will find cats sunning themselves in every campo and calle and you'll probably agree that they are an integral part of the Venetian scene. Most of them look lean and scruffy but they are usually in good health. Dogs are also kept as pets in Venice but they are easily outnumbered by the cats.

Despite the cats, pigeons are plentiful in the Piazza S. Marco where they thrive on the expensive grain bought by well-meaning tourists at the little stands around the piazza.

Remember that rabies exists here as it does in the rest of the European continent.

Banks The main banking areas are around the Piazza S. Marco, Calle Larga XXII Marzo and around the Rialto. Banks are usually open from 0830—1320 and 1445—1545 but they are closed on Saturdays, Sundays and national holidays. There are several Bureaux de Change which are mainly to be found in the same areas as the banks and they are open during shopping hours.

Climate Broadly speaking, the Venetian climate is equable and agreeable. In June, July and August, the average temperature hovers around 24°C (75°F). During January and February, the average daily temperature drops to around 4°C (39°F). There can be heavy rain for long periods in spring and winter. The winter wind comes off the snow covered mountains and is called the *bora* although Venice itself is only rarely covered by snow. The *scirocco* wind comes from Africa and brings hot sticky weather.

Crime Although Italy is notorious for its crime rate, Venice is a relatively safe city. Most Venetians are very honest but, particularly during the high season, it is advisable not to keep all your money in one place and to lock your belongings away. Women should remember that their handbags are popular targets for thieves but, as long as you take reasonable precautions, there is no more need to worry here than anywhere else.

Drinks Venetians, like most Italians, prefer to drink mineral water *(aqua minerale)* with their meals. This is available in two forms — with fizz *(gasata)* and without fizz *(naturale)*. They also enjoy fruit juice *(succo di frutta)* and a great deal of coffee *(caffè)* which they usually take strong and black *(nero)*. If you wish to add milk, this is *cappuccino*. *Macchiato* coffee has a drop of cream in it and *corretto* is served with a drop of brandy. Tea *(tè)* is available but it is not a widely enjoyed beverage in Venice. Hot chocolate *(cioccolata)* is favoured by many Venetians. For more alcoholic beverages, please see p. 20.

Electricity Electric current is 220V AC. Most hotels have the two plug system but carry an adaptor just in case.

Fishing A government permit issued by the Harbourmasters Office is required if you want to fish in certain areas. If you do decide to go fishing, you must be at least 500m away from a beach used by bathers and at least 50m away from fishing installations and ships at anchor.

Hospitals *Civili Riuniti di Venezia*, Campo S.S. Giovanni e Paolo (tel: 705622). *Ospedale al Mare*, Lungomare d'Annunzio, Lido (tel: 761750). In an emergency, dial 113 for ambulance, police or fire. There is first aid available from doctors at airports and railway stations.

Information There are tourist information offices in several parts of Venice. For addresses and telephone numbers, please see p. 29.

Lost Property Railway station (tel: 716122 or 89600). Marco Polo airport (tel: 661266). If you have lost some property in Venice itself, try the Municipio in the Rialto area (tel: 708844). You should also inform the police of any loss, even if you don't think that theft is involved.

Medical Services Emergency — *Unita Sanitaria Locale* keeps a register of doctors and dentists, 3493 Dorsoduro (tel: 708811 in Dorsoduro or 36122 in Castello). Your hotel should also be able to provide you with this information. If you require medicine from a pharmacist at night, go to any pharmacy and you will find information on which are open.

Newspapers English language newspapers are usually available the day after publication. The kiosks in Calle Larga Ascensione behind the Ala Napoleonica and around the Rialto usually have a good selection.

Ospite di Venezia An invaluable publication which is written in both English and Italian. You can find it at tourist offices and hotel desks. Profits go to charity.

Post Office The main post office is in the Fondaco dei Tedeschi by the Rialto (tel: 86212 or 704143).

Railway Station Trains leave from the Stazione Ferrovia S. Lucia (S. Lucia railway station) for Verona, Bologna, Udine and most European capitals. The station has a restaurant, bureau de change and a hotel booking service.

Students There are various special privileges for students — consult the Italian State Tourist Office before departure. For the address of your nearest Italian State Tourist Office, please see p. 29.

Telephones Public telephones, which are quite easy to find, are operated by inserting a coin or a metal disc known as a *gettone*. They can be obtained from post offices, tobacconists and bars.

Toilets There are public toilets at Piazzale Roma, the railway station, the Rialto, the Accademia, and the Albergo Diurno (Day hotel — see Hotels, p. 19). Most cafés, bars and large stores also make toilets available. Men should look for a sign saying *Uomini* or *Signori* and women should look for a sign saying *Donne* or *Signore*. Sometimes a symbol showing a man or a woman is used instead to save confusion.

Venice in Peril Venice is being slowly eroded by the sea from below and pollution from above. The Venice in Peril Fund collects money for the preservation of this unique city.

Water Taxis There are fares laid down for specific runs for a taxi with four passengers. Hired by the hour they are expensive but always negotiate before embarking rather than after your journey is complete.

Zone time Italy is one hour ahead of GMT in summer and six hours ahead of New York time.

Santa Maria della Salute

Sunset on the lagoon

KEY WORDS

Although many Venetians in popular tourist areas speak some English, they always appreciate it when visitors try to speak with them in Italian. In the less popular corners of Venice for tourists, essential phrases can be very useful when asking directions or shopping.

Phrases we list here will not enable you to hold a conversation but they will allow you to communicate better with Venetians and to establish a friendly rapport. When they see you making the effort, they may be even more helpful than usual. It's best to purchase a good Italian phrase book such as Collins Travel Gem size *Italian Phrase Book* and *Italian Dictionary* but some brief guidelines are given below.

Greetings

Formal greetings and handshaking are an essential form of social politeness in Italy. Greetings such as 'good morning' *etc* are used every time you meet someone. They are used as an introduction, say to a question you wish to ask in a shop or restaurant. You are expected to shake hands when you meet anyone with whom you have exchanged more than a few words in the past. For example, it would be polite to shake hands when saying farewell to a hotel concierge with whom you have had a daily conversation.

Greetings are often followed by a mode of address — *signore* (sir) *signora* (madam) or *signorina* (miss).

Words and Phrases

Good morning   *Buon giorno*
Good afternoon/evening   *Buona sera*
Good night   *Buona notte*
Excuse me/sorry   *scusi*
Yes   *sì*
No   *no*
Please   *per favore*
Thank you   *grazie*
You're welcome   *prego*
Pleased to meet you   *Molto lieto*
How are you?   *Come sta?*
Very well, thank you   *Benissimo, grazie*
I don't understand   *Non capisco*
Please speak more slowly   *Parli più lentamente per favore*
Do you speak English?   *Parla inglese?*
Where is . . .?   *Dov'e si trova . . .?*
When?   *Quando?*
What time is it?   *Che ore sono?*
How much?   *Quanto?*
I would like   *Vorrei*
Where is the hotel?   *Dov'e il albergo?*

and   *e, ed*
airport   *aeroporto*
bank   *banca*
bill   *conto*
breakfast   *prima colazione*
bridge   *ponte*
cheap   *a buon mercato*
church   *chiesa*
cold   *freddo -a*
dentist   *dentista*
dinner   *cena*
doctor   *dottore/medico*
exit   *uscita*
expensive   *caro*
ferry crossing   *traghetto*
guide   *cicerone*
hospital   *ospedale*
hot   *caldo -a*

lunch   *pranzo*
market   *mercato*
motorboat   *motoscafo*
museum   *museo*
palace   *palazzo*
park   *parco*
porter   *facchino/portiere*
pharmacy   *farmacia*
post office   *ufficio postale*
station   *stazione*
telephone   *telèfono*
theatre   *teatro*
today   *oggi*
tomorrow   *domani*
tourist office   *Ente del turismo/l'ufficio turistico*
very   *molto*
yesterday   *ieri*

Monday   *lunedì*
Tuesday   *martedì*
Wednesday   *mercoledì*
Thursday   *giovedì*
Friday   *venerdì*
Saturday   *sabato*
Sunday   *domenica*

January   *gennaio*
February   *febbraio*
March   *marzo*
April   *aprile*
May   *maggio*
June   *giugno*
July   *luglio*
August   *agosto*
September   *settembre*
October   *ottobre*
November   *novembre*
December   *dicembre*

Some useful terms when dining out are included on p. 20.

USEFUL ADDRESSES

Before leaving home
Italian State Tourist Office (ENIT)
1 Princes Street, London W1R 8AY (tel:
01-408 1254); 630 Fifth Avenue, Suite
1565, New York NY 10111 (tel: 212-245
4822); 500 North Michigan Avenue, Chicago IL 60611 (tel: 312-644 0990); 360
Post Street, Suite 801, San Francisco 2,
CA 94108 (tel: 415-392 6206); Store 56,
Plaza, 3 Place Ville-Marie, Montreal 113,
Quebec (tel: 514-866 7667); ENIT offices
deal with all enquiries made by intending
travellers to Italy. Once you are in Italy,
your questions will be answered by the
local Tourist Office.
Alitalia UK — 27 Piccadilly, London W1
(tel: 01-759 2510); Alitalia USA — 666
Fifth Avenue, New York (tel: 212-903
3300).

In Venice
Automobile Club d'Italia (ACI),
Fondamenta S. Chiara 518a (tel: 041-
700300).
Italian Touring Club c/o TCI 48/50
Piazza S. Marco (tel: 041-85480). The
TCI issues large scale touring maps and
provides help for foreign motorists in
Italy.
Tourist Offices Calle del Remedio, Cas-
tello 4421 (tel: 041-22373 or 28693); 71c
Calle dell'Ascensione, S. Marco (tel: 041-
26356); 540d Piazzale Roma (summer
only). (Tel: 041-27402); S. Lucia railway
station (tel: 041-715016); Gran Viale,
Lido (tel: 765721).

Consulates
United Kingdom Palazzo Querini,
Accademia, Dorsoduro 1051 (tel: 041-
27207).
United States The nearest consulate is in
Trieste at Via Roma 9, P.O. Box 604.
   As there is no consulate for Australia,
Canada, Eire and New Zealand in the
Venice area, nationals of these countries
would be best advised to contact their
consulate in Rome.
Australia 215 Via Alessandria, Rome
(tel: 06-841241).
Canada 30 Via Zara, Rome (tel: 06-
864101).
Eire 108 Via del Pozzetto, Rome (06-
6782541).
New Zealand 2 Via Zara, Rome (06-
8448663).

Churches
Services are usually held in Italian.
Anglican St. George's, Campo S. Vio,
Dorsoduro.
Greek Orthodox Ponte dei Greci, Cas-
tello.
Jewish Synagogue Ghetto Vecchio,
Cannaregio.
Lutheran Campo S.S. Apostoli, Can-
naregio.
Methodist Campo S. Maria Formosa,
Castello.
Roman Catholic Most churches includ-
ing Basilica of S. Marco, Piazza S. Marco.
There is occasionally a service in English
at the church of S. Moisè in S. Marco.

Useful telephone numbers
Emergency (ambulance, police, fire) 113;
Carabinieri (local police) 32222; Passport
office 703222 or 700754.
   Railway (Sta Lucia Station) 715555;
Airport (Marco Polo) 661111.
   Hospital *(Civili Reuniti di Venezia),*
Campo S.S. Giovanni e Paolo, Castello
(tel: 705622); Ospedale (hospital) al
Mare, Lido (tel: 760180); Unita Sanitaria
Locale (for doctor and dentists register)
(tel: 708811).
   Dialling code for Venice from United
Kingdom: 010 3941. Dialling code for
Venice from United States and Canada:
011 3941.

FESTIVALS AND EVENTS

There are several traditional events in Venice such as the *Carnevale, Vogalonga, Festa del Redentore etc* which have become the great showpieces of the year, attracting an international following but there are also many other festivals or shows of a more local character. Information about these, as well as the big events, can be found in the free *Ospite di Venezia* (see p. 27) or in the local newspaper or at the Tourist Information Office.

The first big event of the year is the *Carnevale*, a modern revival of the great Mardi Gras festivals of the 18th century. *Carnevale* takes place the week before Lent and, as in the past, there are galas, music, dancing and general fun in the streets where many people appear in costume and disguise themselves with colourful masks. Hotels hold gala nights, theatrical events are staged and music is heard everywhere.

On the first Sunday after Ascension Day, the day when the Doges used to throw a ring into the Adriatic as a symbol of Venice's marriage to the sea, there is a marathon row around Venice called the *Vogalonga* (long row). The route begins at the lagoon in front of the Doges Palace and continues via S. Elena and Burano to the Fondamente Nuove. The route then turns down the Canal di Cannaregio and the Canal Grande, finishing at the Dogana. Gondolas, rowing boats, skiffs, rafts and any vessel propelled by hand can take part. The marathon starts at 0930 and it is 20 miles (32 km) long.

Every second year in June (even years) the largest modern art exhibition in the world, known as the *Biennale*, takes place. Works are exhibited in buildings in the Palazzo Pubblico and other galleries such as those of the Arsenale. During this period, many of the city's private galleries put on their own shows and concerts, theatre performances and other events are laid on for the visitors arriving from all over the world for this important event.

Film actors and crew in the Piazza

The *Festa del Redentore*, which takes place on the third Sunday in July, is the most spectacular event of the Venetian year. A bridge of boats is built from Dorsoduro to the church of the Redentore on Giudecca and Venetians and visitors flock across the 'bridge' to the island. In the evening, the lagoon is filled with every kind of boat, loaded with excited passengers happily eating and drinking (hotels put on their own boat services for this event) and everyone has a good time. The moment that everyone is waiting for is the huge firework display which lights up the night sky in the dramatic style characteristic of Italian firework displays. After the final crescendo, those who have any energy left head for the Lido where a great deal of coffee is consumed and a few keep up the tradition of a quick dip in the Adriatic.

The *International Film Festival* takes place in August/September at the Palazzo del Cinema on the Lido. The hotels, here, live up to the reputations of their scintillating guests by putting on special festive arrangements. Venice is thronged with stars of film and television during the two weeks of the festival and you may catch sight of one or two of them among the tourists who throng the Piazza S. Marco at this popular time of year.

In autumn, the festivities take on a more sedate tempo as the season of music and opera begins. One of the pleasures of the Musical Fortnight, which usually takes place in September, is that you can listen to the music of Albinoni, Monteverdi and Vivaldi in the kind of settings for which it was composed.

September is the month of another major spectacle on the Canal Grande — the *Regata Storica*. A wonderful procession of Venetian boats with their rowers in historical costume opens the proceedings which include various races between gondolas and other craft.

The festive year ends with the *Festa della Madonna*, the focal point of which is the procession to the church of S. Maria della Salute across two floating bridges over the Canal Grande.

During the winter, cultural life continues with opera, music, theatre and art exhibitions until the spring when festival time comes round again.

The Canal Grande

Five bridges over the Rio di Palazzo

Venice City Maps

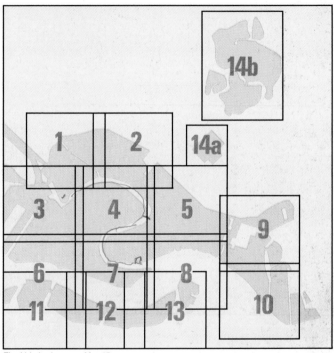

The Lido is shown as Map 15

Key to Symbols

———— Railway	🅿 🅿	Multi-storey car park / Car park
Shipping route / Boat tour	ℹ️ 🅿	Tourist information / Police
Landing	✉ TAXI	Post Office / Taxi
—17— Car Ferry	Ⓣ Ⓖ	Taxi boat / Gondola
Public building / Sight	✈	Airport
Park / Sportsground		

These maps are adapted with kind permission from the Hallwag city map series
© Wm. Collins, Sons & Co. Ltd.

E

F

1

Canale

Fondamenta della Sacca

Calle 1/a Case Nuove

Calle Lunga d. Penitenti

Corte delle Case Nuove

C. Luig.

Luzzat.

Cpl. d.

Cent.

Calle le Case Nuove

Calle Nuove

Calle del Forner

Sacca di S. Girolamo

Corte Giustiniana

Corte Ferau

Campiello de

Calle e le Cooperative

Calle delle Cooperative

Fondamenta di San

Fondamenta

Canale di San

2

Pte. d. Tre Archi

✉

Calle dell' Angelo

Bar Pa

Srl

Calle 1. d. Beccarie

Cpl. delle Corte Beccarie Balleran

Corte Gonnella

C. d. Magazzen

Calle del Braccio

Ct Braccio Nudo

Cpl. della Grana

Cpl. delle Beccarie

Beccarie delle

Calle del Chiodi

Cpl. Ca Pesaro

Calle delle

Ponte Saponello

Giobbe

Ponte Tre Archi

Fondamenta

Cort

Calle Calle delle

C Calle larga del lavander

C. d. San

Calle del Scariatto

C. dei Colori

C. del Vino

C. del Colori

Calle del Verde

Campo di S. Giobbe

Chiesa di S. Giobbe

Calle del Ospitale

Calle Biscottella

C. d. Blancheria

Ceseria

della

Calle di San

Cpl. d. Pazienza

Chiesa di Pazienza

R. terra d

Calle

Rio di

Campo Bosello

Crea

della

Canale

della

Rio della

Crea

Calle

Calle Priuli

detta

3

© Hallwag A.G.Bern

E

F P

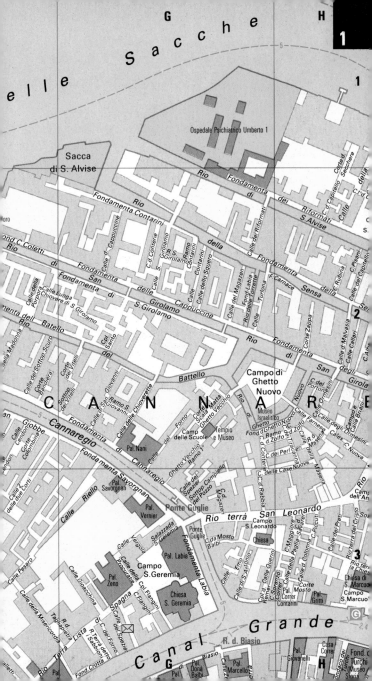

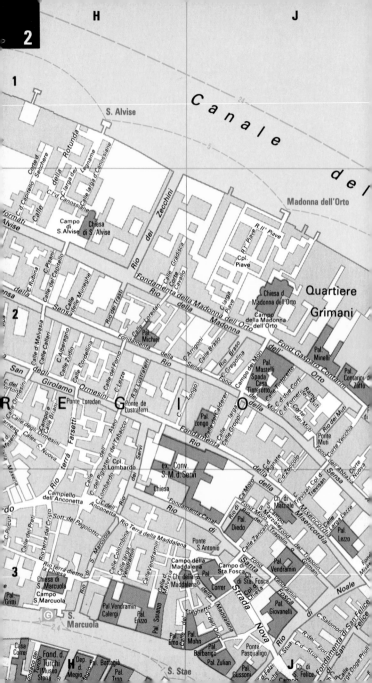

2

H   J

1

C a n a l e

S. Alvise

d e l

Madonna dell'Orto

Cortal d. Secchere
Calle d. Capitello
Calle della Rotunda
Cl. larga de Legname
Calle larga dei Carrossiane
Cl.d Canossiane

Rio dei Zecchini

Campo di S.Alvise
Chiesa di S. Alvise

R II° Piave
R I° Piave

Cpl. Piave

C. Pisani
Calle del Capitello
C. Rubina

Calle Gradisca
Calle Cavallo
Corte Cavallo

della
Sensa

Calle della Muneghe
Rio de Trasti
Calle Loredan

Fondamenta della Madonna dell'Orto

Rio della

Campo della Madonna dell'Orto
Chiesa d. Madonna dell'Orto

Quartiere

2

Calle di Malvasia
Calle Cafari
C.Albergano
Calle Zudio
Pal. Michiel
Fondamenta
Calle del Forno
Calle Cordellina

della

Rio

Madonna

C.Arrigoni
Calle Braso
Rio Sensa
Rio Gregolina
Rio Braso

Campo dei Mori

Pal. Mastelli
Casa Spada
Casa Tintoretto
C.d. due Corti
C.d Forneri dei Muti
Fondta. dei Mori
Corte Tintoretto
Corte dei Muti

Fond. Gasparo Contarini

Pal. Minelli

Pal. Contarini d. Zaffo

Grimani

San
C. del Ortondo

degli
C.Ormesini
Calle degli Ormesini
Calle Briani
C. Brazzo

Girolamo Ormesini
Calle C. Nuova
Ponte Loredan

Farsetti
Calle C.Lezze
R.d Lustraferi
Ponte de Lustraferi

dell'

Rio di Lustraferi

Pal. Longo
Calle larga
Calle Groppi
dei Caldereri

R E G I O

dell'

Orto

Rio dei Muti
Ponte Vecchio
Ponte Muti
Corte Vecchia
Corte Abbazia
Corte Nuova

C.Calle degli Ormesini
C.Masena
Masena
Calle C. Nuova

R E G I O

Rio terrà Farsetti

Calle dell'Aseo
Calle dei Servi

Rio Terrà del Tabacco
Fondamenta

Rio

della

C.d Pignate
C.d Foscolo
C.Trevisan Cpl d. Trevisan

Misericordia
Larga Lezze

Cpl. Lombardo
C. del Pignater
C.dell'Lombardo
C.C.dell'Anconetta

della

Sensa

Corte Misericordia

Campiello dell'Anconetta
Sott. del Pegolotto

ex. Conv.
S. M. d. Servi

Chiesa

Ca. Mora

Ch. di Marziale
Fond. Moro
Rio del Moro
Fond.S.Marziale
Tragh. di Marcilian
Fond. dei Tagnoli
Grimani

Pal. Lezze

C.Calle dei Preti
C.Cloccuri
do
Rio terrà del Cristo

Rio Terrà della Maddalena

Calle Colombina
Calle larga Vendramin

Rio di

Fondamenta Canal di

Pal. Diedo

Calle Zancani

Fond. della
Misericordia
C. Marcona

Pal. Misterio

Chiesa di S.Marcuola
Campo S.Marcuola

Ponte S. Antonio

Campo della Maddalena
Ch. della Maddalena

Pal.

Campo di Sta. Fosca
Ch. di Sta. Fosca

Santa

Fond.

Pal. Vendramin

Pal. Vendramin
Calle Vendramin
C.d Maddalena

Correr
Strada

Calle d Malvasia
della
Maddalena

Pal. Giovanelli

Fosca

Pal.
Gritti
Pal. Vendramin Calergi

Pal. Enzzo

G

S.
Marcuola

3

Rio di S. Marcuola
Calle larga Vendramin
Rio di

Rio del

Maddalena

Nova

Noale

Rio di

C.Salomon di San Felice
R. dei Forni
Fondamenta San Felice
Ch. di

Casa Correr
Fond. d. Turchi
Museo Storia

Dep. d.
Megio
Pal. Battaggiè
Pal. Tron.

Pal. Erno
Pal. Mohn

Ponte Pasqualigo

Pal. Barbango
Pal. Zulian
Pal. Gussoni

C. Stua
C.d. Stua
C. Stua

Traghetto
S. Felice
S. Felice

H

S. Stae

J

Correr

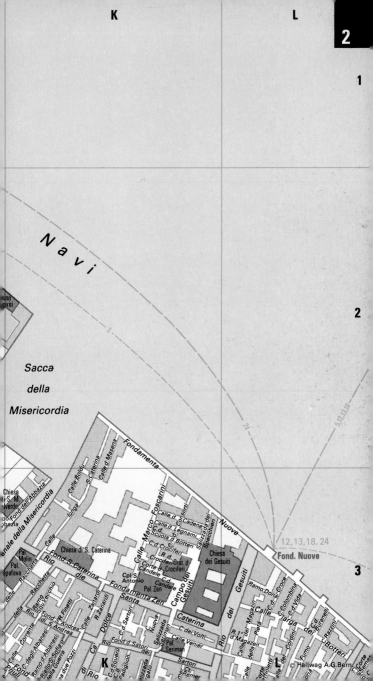

K L

2

1

2

3

N a v i

sino
piriti

Sacca

della

Misericordia

Fondamenta

Canale della Misericordia

Chiesa
i S. M.
alverde
o Fond. dell'Abbazia
bbazia

Pal.
Molin
Pal.
apafava

Chiesa di S. Caterina

Calle Boldu

Calle d. Masena

S. Caterina

Calle lunga

Calle

Racchetta

Fond. S. Caterina
die

Rio

Pal.
Racchetta

Foscarini

Calle d. S. Cadene

Calle d. Legnami

C. d. Botteri

Scuola d.

C.d. Crociferi

Crociferi

Corte d. Crociferi

C. d. Candele

Candele

Foscarini

Salizzada dei Specchieri

Nuove

Oråt. d.

R.d.

C. d.

Fondamenta Zen

Cpl.S.
Antonio

Pal. Zen

Campo dei
Gesuiti

Chiesa
dei Gesuiti

Fondamenta

Santa

Caterina

Gesuiti

Rio dei

C. Vecchio

C. S.Queuro

Fond. S.M.
Finetti

Ramo

Zanardi

Fond.

R.Zanardi

C.d. Sartori

Nuova

Fond. d'Albanesi
S. Andrea

R. d' Andrea

Ramo d'Albanesi

R.tio S.Sofia

Fond. d. Sartori

Salizzada

Sartori

C. d. Volti

Calle Venier

Pal.
Seriman

Ramo Donà

Croce

Calle

C. Colombina

C. d.rida

Calle

larga

dei

C. Burnelli

C. Razzini

Ramo

C.Botteri

C. d. Magazen

Calle d.rimini

Piete

C.Rizzetti

C. d. Cordini

Calle

delle

Corte

Scrime

Chiaro

12,13,18,24

Fond. Nuove

K L

© Hallwag A.G.Bern

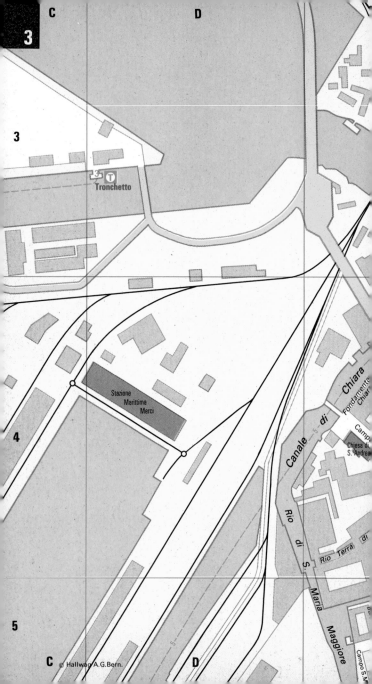

3

3

T Tronchetto

4

Stazione Marittima Merci

Chiara

Canale di

Fondamenta Chiara

Camp

Chiesa di S. Andrea

Rio di S.

Rio Terra di

5

Maria

Maggiore

Campo S. M.

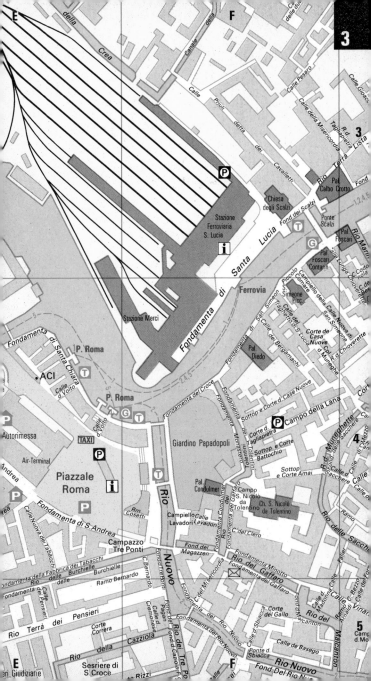

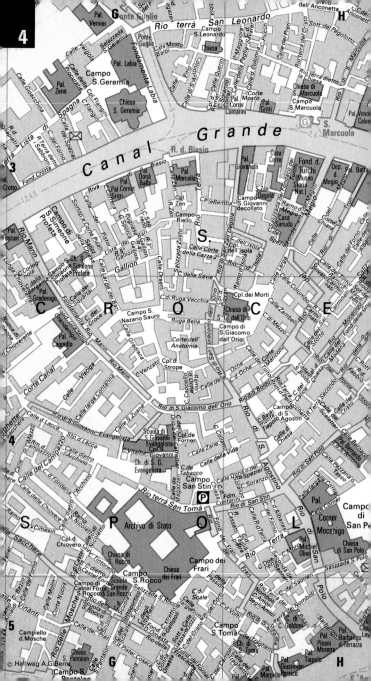

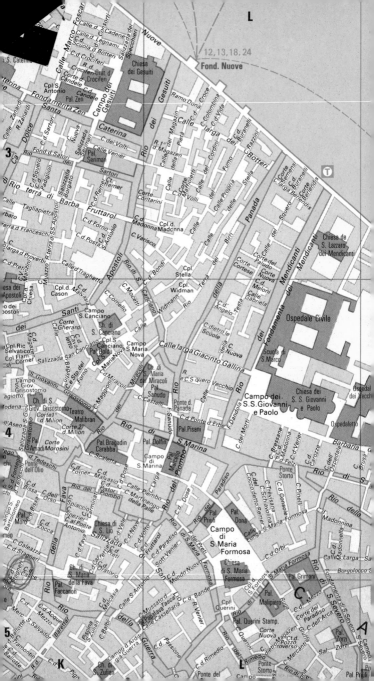

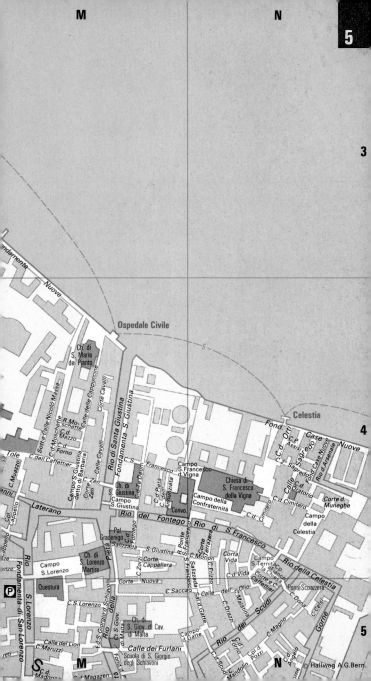

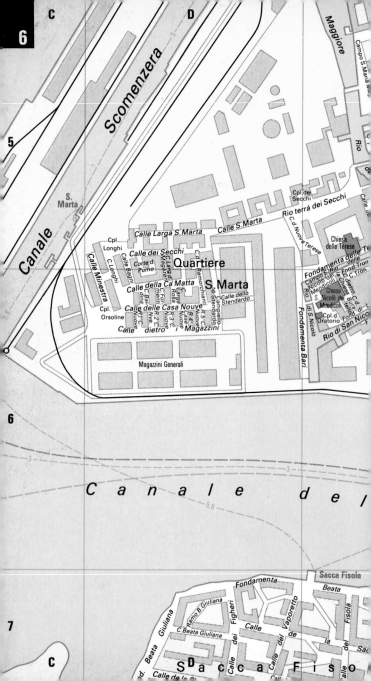

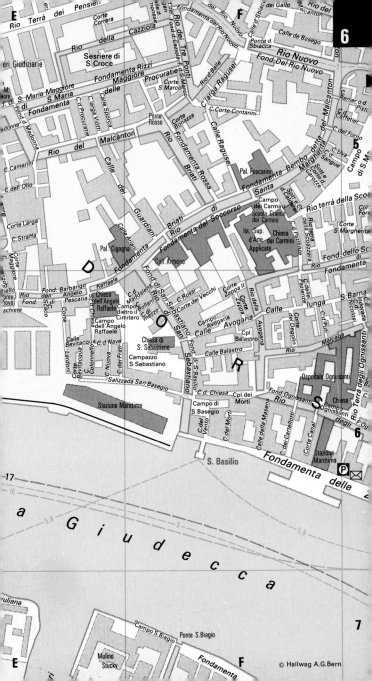

Rio Terrà dei Pensieri
Corte Correra
Rio dei Tre Ponti
Corte Cazziola
del
Rio del
Rio del Gallo
del Galletti
di Sbiacca
Calle de Basego
Ponte d.
Sbiacca
Rio Nuovo
Fond. Del Rio Nuovo
C. d. Renier o d.
C. d. Caffetier
C. del Forno

Fondamenta del Rio Nuovo
C. d. Fondamenta de' Garzoti
C. d. S. Marco
Sesriere di
S. Croce
Fondamenta Rizzi
Maggiore
Procuratie
Corte
S. Marco
C. l.arga Ragusei

eri Giudiziarie
J. di S. Maria Maggiore
S. Maria
Fondamenta
delle
Procuratie
C. d Procuratie
C.l.arga Viotti
Calle Sporca
Ponte
Rosso
Corte
Bonazza
Calle Ragusei
C. Corte Contarini
Campo
di S. M.

M.
fore
donna
Fond. d'Madonna
Rio
della
Rio del Malcanton
Calle dei Guardiani
Fondamenta
Rossa
Briati
di
Pal. Foscarini
Fondamenta Bembo detta del Malcanton
Santa
Margherita
C. d. Uva
Sotto e
Sopra il C.
C. Croze
5

C. Camerini
C. dell'Olio
Corte Larga
C. Straffa
Corte Maggiore
Pal. Cigogna
Coll. Armeno
Briati
Rio
Fondamenta del Soccorso
Campo
dei Carmini
Scuola Grande
dei Carmini
Ist. Sup.
d'Arte dei Carmini
Applicate.
Rio terrà della Scoa
Rio terrà della Scoazzera
C. d. Pazienze
Corte
S. Margherita
Fond. dello Sc
di
Fondamenta

iello
nova
chiera
Fond. dell'
Angelo
Barbarigo
Pescaria
di
Fond.
Raffaele
Chiesa
dell'Angelo
Raffaele
Campo
dell'Angelo
Raffaele
C. d.
Maddalena
C. d.
Bottani
Fond. di San Sebastiano
C. Rossi
C. d. mezzo
Corte de' Vecchi
Calle
Corte
Zappa II
Corte
Zappa
Rio della
Calle
Calle
del Degolin
Corte
Pazienze
lunga
S. Barna
C. d. Putti
C. d. Indrada
S. Nicolos
D

Rio
Fond.
Corte
Calle Bevilacqua
Chiesa
dietro il
Cimitero
Calle Colombine
C. Nuova
C. dei Frati
Chiesa di
S. Sebastiano
Campo
Avogaria
Calle
Avogaria
Cpl.
Balastro
Calle
Avogaria
O
R

Calle Lardoni
Corte
Bevilacqua
Salizzada San Basegio
Campazzo
S. Sebastiano
C. di S. Basilio
Calle di San Sebastiano
Calle Balastro
Cpl. dei
Morti
Malcaga
Ospedale Ognissanti
Chiesa
Campo
Ognissanti
degli
Rio Terrà degli Ognissanti
S

Stazione Marittima
C. d. Vento
C. dei Morti
Campo di
S. Basegio
C. d. Chiesa
Calle della Masena
Fond. Ognissanti
Rio
Corte Cartellotti
Rio Canal
Fondamenta delle
Stazione
Marittima
P
6

S. Basilio
Fondamenta
delle

17
16
5,8
a
5,8
G i u d e c c a
3
5,8

iuliana
Campo S. Biagio
Ponte S. Biagio
Mulino Stucky
Fondamenta

E
F
© Hallwag A.G.Bern
7

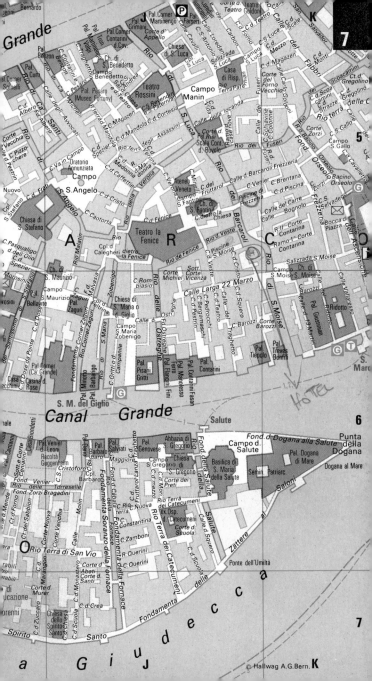

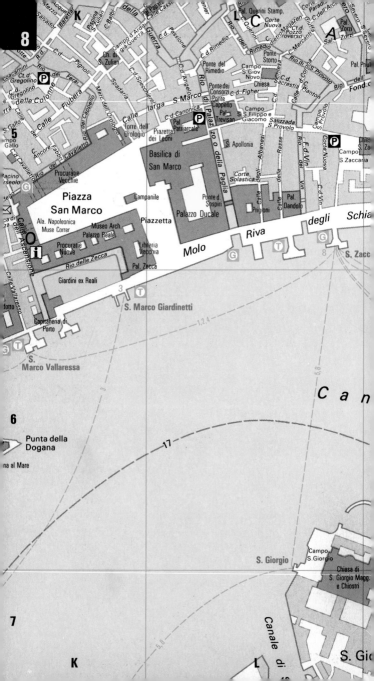

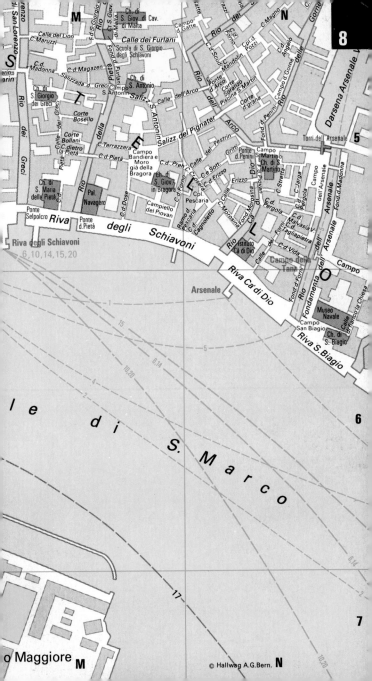

Ch. di
S. Giov. di Cav.
di Malta

M
Calle del Lion
C. Maruzzi

F. di S. Giorgio
Rio

Ch. di
S. Giov.

Calle dei Furlani

Campo
di Gatte

Rio
C. d. Forno

C. Magno
Col.

N

Gorne

Scuola di S. Giorgio
degli Schiavoni

S
Calle d.
Madonna

C. d.
Magazen

Salizzada d. Greci

Fond. di Furlani

Ch. di
S. Antonio
S. Antonin

C. d. Scuola

C. Mandolin

C. d.
Pozzi

C. d.
Angelo

Col.
d. Forno

arin

Ch. di
S. Giorgio
dei Greci

C. d. dei Greci

Salizz. S. Antonin

Salizz. del Pignater

Calle dell'Arco

Ponte
d'Arco

Corte
Soranzo

Campo d.
Arco

Fond. d. Penini

Campo d Gorne delle

Darsena Arsenale

Rio
dei
Greci

Corte
Bosello

della

Pietà

C. d. dietro
la Pietà

C. Terrazzera

Campo
Bandiera e
Moro
già della
Bragora

Calle de' Pestrin

Calle del
Fond.

Ch. di
S. Antonin

Piscina
S. Martin

Corte
d'grana

Torri dell'Arsenale

5

Ch. di
S. Maria
della Pietà

Corte
Bollani

C. d. Pietà

C. d. Preti

C. C.

C. e Sott.

Gritti
Ponte
d. Penini

Erizzo

Campo
S. Martino

Ch. di S
Martino

C. d.
Larga

Campo
dell'Arsenale

Fond. d. Madonna

Pal.
Navagero

Rio

C. d. Dose

Ch. di
S. Giov.
in Bragora

C. C.

C. d. Enzzo

C. Pescaria

Cpl.

Dio

C. Stretta

C. d.
Pergola

C. d.
Pergola

Arsenale

Ponte
Selpolcro

Riva

Ponte
d. Pietà

Riano d.
Pescaria

Calle
Cagnoletto

C. Morosina

Fond. Morosina

Cà

C. d.
Malvasia

C. d.
Fortagliapietra

dell' Arsenale

Campo

Riva degli Schiavoni

degli Schiavoni

Riva degli Schiavoni
6, 10, 14, 15, 20

Istituto
Cà di Dio

Calle de
Cà di Dio

C. d. Vida

L

Campo della
Tana

Fond. d. Forni

Rio

Fondamenta dell' Arsenale

Calle
dietro la Chiesa

Campo

O

Museo
Navale

Arsenale

Riva Cà di Dio

Campo
San Biagio

Ch. di
S. Biagio

Riva S. Biagio

– 1

15

5

6, 14

10, 20

o Maggiore   **M**

4

2

l   e   d   i   S.   M   a   r   c   o

6

17

6, 14

10, 20

© Hallwag A.G. Bern.   **N**

7

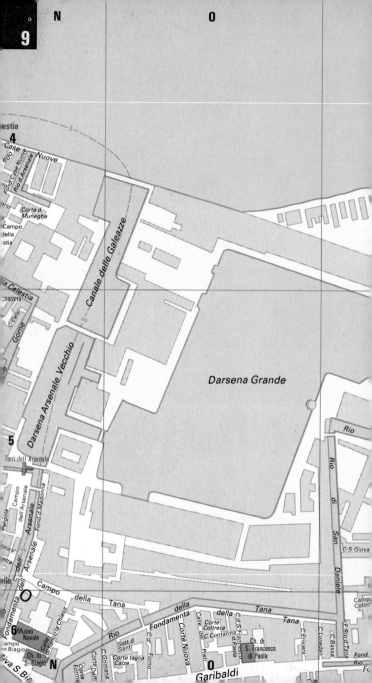

P   Q   1

Campo Sportivo

Bacini di Cannareggio

4

Canale di Porta Nuova

5

le

Vergini

ampo
aniele

S.Daniele

C.larga S.Pietro

C.d
igher

C.d·Terco

Campo
di
San Pietro

Ch. di
S. Pietro
di Castello

pl di
garetto

C.d
Campo
di Ruga

C.Marafani

C.d·Ole

porca

C.Salamon

C·Riello

Corte del
Bianco

C.d. Ponte S.Anna
Corte Caparozzo

C S.Anna

S. Pietro

Fond Quintavalle

Corte Nova

C. d·larga Quintavalle

Cpl dei Vigna

C.

Calle di Mezzo

Fond·Castel· Olivolo

Canale di San

Pietro

C Quinta-
valle

Cpl dei
Pomeri

C.d·Farti

6

chino
di
enta

Rialto
Fornet

di

P S.Anna
Ch.
di S. Anna

S.Anna

di Quintavalle

Q

© Hallwag A.G.Bern.

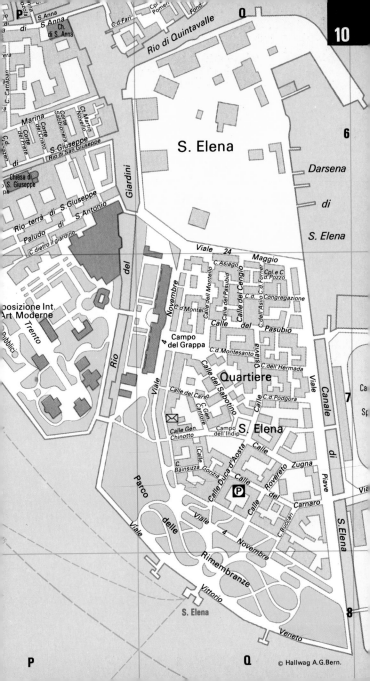

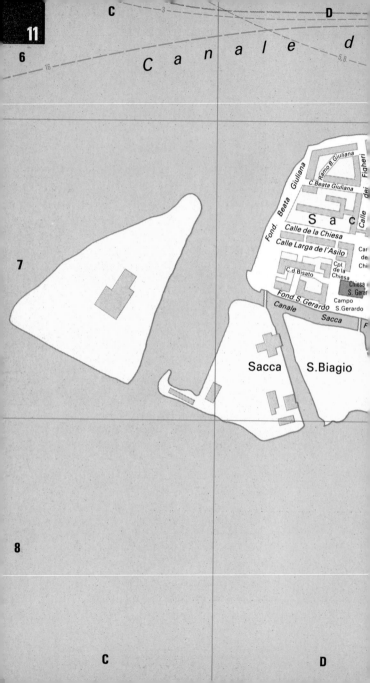

C

D

C a n a l e d

C a n a l e

16

3

5,8

7

Fond. Beata Giuliana

C.Beata Giuliana

Ramo B. Giuliana

Calle dei Figheri

S a c

Calle de la Chiesa

Calle Larga de l'Asilo

Calle dei

C.d Bisato

Cpl. de la Chiesa

Car de Chi

Chiesa S. Gerar

Campo S.Gerardo

Fond S.Gerardo

Canale   Sacca

F

Sacca

S.Biagio

8

C

D

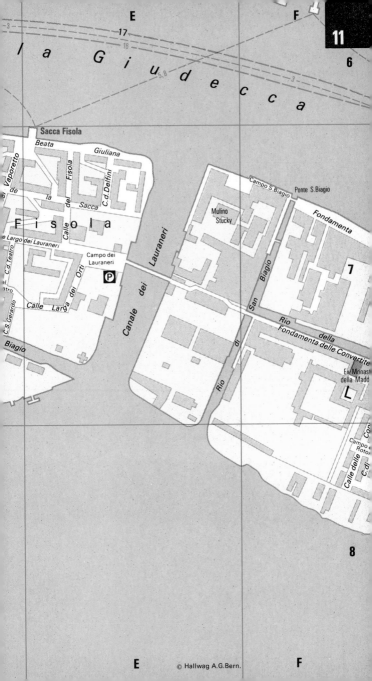

la Giudecca

3
17
16
5,8
3

Sacca Fisola

Beata

Giuliana

C.d.Delfini

Calle del la Fisola

Sacca

F i s o l a

Vaporetto

de

la

e Largo dei Lauraneri

C.d.Teatro

C.S.Gerardo

Campo dei
Lauraneri

Calle a dei Orti

P

Calle Larga

Biagio

Lauraneri

Canale dei

Rio di

Rio

Mulino
Stucky

Campo S.Biagio

Ponte S.Biagio

Fondamenta

San

Biagio

Rio

della

Fondamenta delle Convertite

Ex Monast
della Madd

L

Campo
Roto

Calle delle

C. di

Con

12

6

7

8

S. Basilio **F**

Stazione
Marittima

Calle Trevisan

Fondamenta delle Zattere

Fond. Bonlini

Ognissanti **G**

Corte
Colomb

S. Trovaso

Campo
S. Trovaso

San

D

C.e Ct.d.
Magazen

Rio

C.d Frati

Chies

Zattere

Fondam

C a n a l e

d e l l

3

5,8

16

17

5,8

3

9,10

8,9

S. Biagio

Ponte S.Biagio

Fondamenta

San

Biagio

S. Eufemia

Fondamenta

Chiesa
di S. Eufemia

San

Eufemia

9

Giu

Rio
Fondamenta delle Convertite

Convertite

Fond. di San Eufemia

Corte Nuove

Campazzo S. Cosmo

Calle Montorio

Calle d. Pestor

Accademia

dei

Nobili

Calle dei Nicoli

Calle del Forno

Ex Monastero
della Maddalena

L

Campo di
San Cosmo

San

A

Chiesa
di
S. Cosmo

Corte dei
Cordami

Calle

del Forno

Calle dei Spini

P

Piccolo

Corte
Ferraro

Campo della
Rotonda

Convertite

C.di Mezzo

C. del

Rio della di Rotonda

Fond. della

Lunga

Calle

del

Corte
Grande

G

Calle

del

Ponte

Rio

Calle d.

I

Calle dei

Canticre

L

Calle

Camp di
Dentro

F. Berlomoni

Rio

Corte
Berlomoni

P

L *a* **G**

F **G**

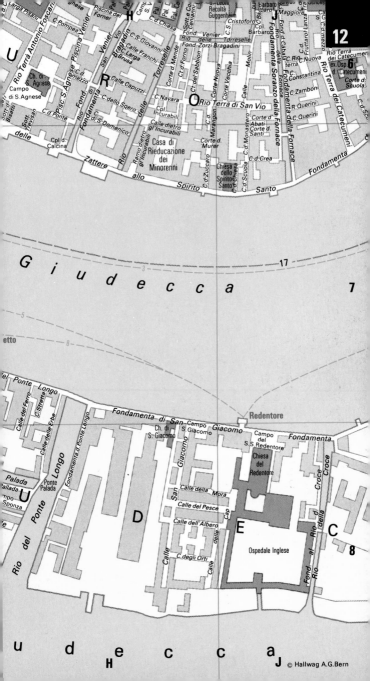

13

Campo Chiesa
S.Gregorio di S.Gregorio
C.d.Mori Corte dei Preti
C.Rio Nuova
Fondamenta della Salute
Basilica di S.Maria della Salute
Pal. Dogana di Mare **K**
Dogana al Mare
Semin. Patriarc.
J
Saloni
C.Constantina
R.Querini
Corte d. Scuola
Rio Terra dei Catecumeni ex.Osp.
C.d.Catecumeni
C.Zamboni
C.Querini
Salute
Calle d.Squero
Rio Terra dei Catecumeni
Zattere
Ponte dell'Umiltà
Fondamenta Soranzo della Fornace
Fondamenta della Fornace
C.Rio terra
Fondamenta
delle
6
7
17
3

C a n a l e   d e l l a
5,8

Zitelle
Fond. delle
Chiesa delle
Zit
O

Croce

della

Chiesa della Croce

Fondamenta
Croce
Croce
Rio d.Croce
Rio al
Fond.al
e Inglese
8

C   **C**

A

Calle

Calle del Gran
Ramo d.Gran
Ramo d.Squero
Calle del
C.larga d.Cooperativa
Calle dei Saon

C.dell'asilo Mas
C.3°
C.2°Campalto
Calle 2°
Michelangelo

Squero

ntore
 entore
po
fre

J   **K**

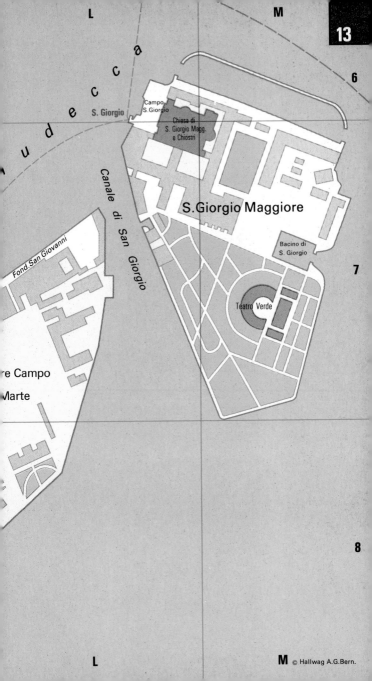

L

M

6

dé cc a

Giudecca

S. Giorgio

Campo
S.Giorgio

Chiesa di
S. Giorgio Magg.
e Chiostri

S.Giorgio Maggiore

Canale di San Giorgio

Fond.San Giovanni

Bacino di
S. Giorgio

7

re Campo

Marte

Teatro Verde

8

L

M © Hallwag A.G.Bern.

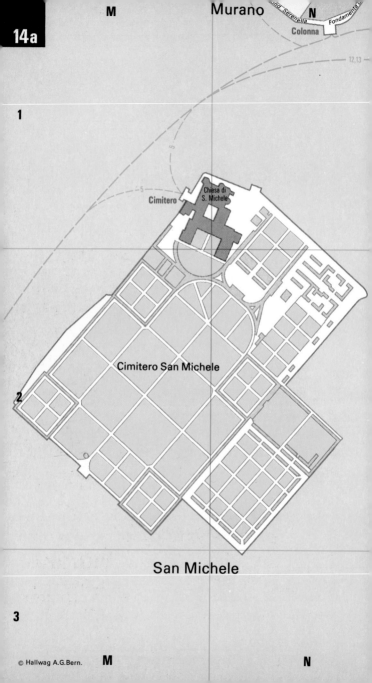

Colonna

12,13

1

5

5

Cimitero

Chiesa di
S. Michele

Cimitero San Michele

2

San Michele

3

M

N

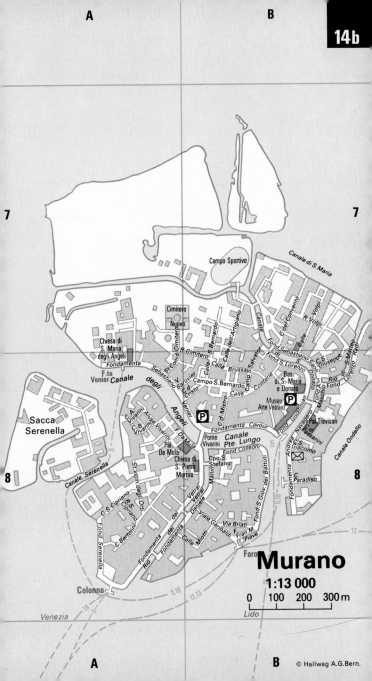

14b

A B

7 7

Campo Sportivo

Canale di S. Maria

Cimitero
Nuovo

R. Volpi
C. del Convento
Fond. Sebastiano Santonato

Chiesa di
S. Maria
degli Angeli
Fondamenta
F.ta
Venier Canale degli Angeli

R. Cimitero
St C.d Cimitero
Calle del Artigiano
Calle S. Bernardo
Calle
Brussad
Fond. S Lorenzo
Calle
R. Volpi
di S. Giuseppe
S. Matteo

St C.d Cimitero
S. Sebastiano

V.
Barovier
Calle d
Cristo
Campo S. Bernardo
Campo Salvator
Conterie
Bas.
di S. Maria
e Donato

Rio di S.
Lorenzo Rio
Fond. Lorenzo

Sacca
Serenella

Canale Serenella

A.
Vivarini
Alvise Vivarini
C. B.
Vivarini
F. D. Mula

Pal.
Da Mula
Chiesa di
S. Pietro
Martire

St Vicin degli Orti

Fondamenta Cavour
Museo
Arte Vetraio

Ponte
Vivarini
Canale
Pte. Lungo
Fond. Colleoni
Cpo. S.
Stefano

Fond. Andrea Navagero Giustinian

Pal. Trevisan
Passerini
C. Giacomo

C. Paradiso

Canale Ondello

8 8

C. S. Cipriano
B. S.
Cipriano

C. Bertolini

Fond. Serenella
Fond.
Rio

Fondamenta
del
Fondamenta
Calle Miotti

Vetrai
Vetrai
Daniele
Manin

V.le Garibaldi
Via Briati
Fran M.
Piave

Fond. S. Giov. dei Battuti

5.18

12
13

Colonna

5.18
12,13
18
5

Faro

Murano

1:13 000

0 100 200 300 m

Venezia

Lido

A B

© Hallwag A.G. Bern.

P

Lazzaretto
Vecchio

Q

L a g u n a

V. Lemno

V. Navarrino

V. Pirano

Riva   di   Corinto

V. Rodi

V. D. Selva

Via   Sandro

V. Lorenzo

Marcello

V. Morosini

V. A. Lamberti

Campo sportivo

Gallo

V. d'Acri

G.   Lepanto

Via J. Nani

Chiesa
Sant'Antonio

Sandro

V. Fratt. Morosini

V. Candia

Via

Via

G.   Via

Marc.

3 Via

V. Lepanto

V. A. Emo

Palazzo
del Cinema

Casino
Municipale

Via Quattro fontane

Via

V. Istria

Lungomare G. Marconi

Lungomare

V. Dalmazia

Pza
Fiume

D.

Marco

G.

Lido di Venezia

© Hallwag A.G.Bern.

M a r e

San Giorgio Maggiore

Lido
Chiesa S. Maria
Elisabetta

R   V   e   n   e   t   a   S

Tempio Votivo

Lido
S. Nicolò

San   Nicolò

Riviera   Cimitero
                          Cattolico   Campo
                                          sportivo
V. Negroponte   V. Morea
                  V.   V. Marco Polo   Aeroporto
V. Smirne   G. Nicelli
V. Scutari   Via Tiro   Cipro
                                    Cimitero
Via Zara   Israelitico
          Via   Rovigno   Via
Via   C. Zano Cipro
V. Famagosta   Via   Parenzo
                  Pza
                  Pola
Piazzale   Via Dietro l'Ospizio Marino   Piazzale
Bucintoro   R. Ravà
          Lungomare G. D'Annunzio
                          Ospedale a Mare
Terrazza
a Mare

                              Bagni Comunali comunali
                              1:14500

r   i   a   t   i   c   o   0   200   400 m

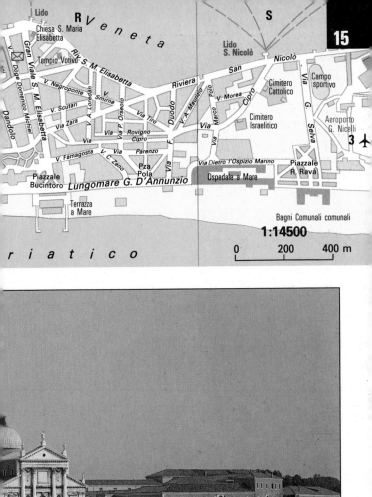

The Piazza at night, during the day and from the air

MUSEUMS AND GALLERIES

Map references refer to the maps on pp. 33–63.

With its wealth of palazzi and churches which are no longer used for their original purpose, Venice is not short of space for exhibitions of art, furniture, clothing and other museum items. Venice has accumulated one of the greatest collections of treasure held by any city on earth. When in its prime, the Republic gathered many treasures to add to its wealth and, even during the centuries when it was in decline, Venice attempted to boost its failing confidence by collecting as much as it could.

Opening hours Museums are open most days but they are usually closed on main holidays. Most are closed on Jan 1, Easter, May 1, Aug 15, and Christmas but they are open at weekends. There is usually an entrance fee to pay but on certain days you may get in free. Opening times given here are for the summer season. In winter, most places are open for a shorter period each day. It's best not to plan too far ahead as opening times are often changed without any apparent reason. You will also find that certain museum rooms are sometimes closed to the Public without notice.

Accademia Belle Arti e Galleria (Academy), Campiello della Carità, Dorsoduro (tel: 52 22247). Opening times: Tues, Wed, Thu, Fri, Sat 0900–1400; Sun 0900–1300. Closed Mon. Admission is free on the 1st and 4th Sat of each month and 1st and 3rd Sun.

This major Venetian art gallery is located south of the city by the Canal Grande. It is now on the site of the old church of La Carità which is depicted with a tower in a Canaletto painting held by London's National Gallery. The campanile fell down in 1744 but some of the original building remains in rooms XXIII and XXIV.

The roughly chronological arrangement of the rooms in the Accademia gives you the opportunity to study the development of art styles from the 14th to the 18th century. A brief description of each room is given here.

Room I This was originally the assembly room of the scuola (guild) and it has a fine wooden ceiling by Marco Cozzi.

The paintings are mostly Venetian Primitives from the 14th and early 15th centuries. They were part of a collection owned by Giambattista Piazzetta, a painter who was also the first President of the Academy.

Among the paintings in this room you can view the *Coronation of the Virgin*, a polyptych with other scenes from the lives of Christ and St Francis. The *Annunciation with Saints and Prophets*, painted by Lorenzo Veneziano in 1357, is one of the most important works of its time.

Room II The transition from primitive to more sophisticated work in this room is sudden. It contains excellent paintings by Giovanni Bellini and the incomparable Carpaccio. Giovanni Bellini was the pioneer of Venetian style which flowered in the work of Giorgione and Titian, both pupils of the Bellini studio.

Giovanni Bellini's altarpiece, *Madonna Enthroned with Saints*, was painted in the 1480s after he had met Antonello da Messina and was evolving away from the style which he had learned from Mantegna. Carpaccio's altarpiece, the *Presentation of Jesus*, was painted in 1510, soon after he had worked as assistant to Giovanni Bellini and it bears a certain resemblance to the Bellini altarpiece.

Room III Smaller paintings by followers of Giorgione fill this room.

Room IV Bellini's brother-in-law and earliest influence was Mantegna whose painting, *St George*, is an important feature of this room. Although *St George* is a small painting its statuesque quality attracts many of the Accademia's visitors. Also in this room, there is an early Piero della Francesca work — *St Jerome*, and Cosmè Tura's *Madonna of the Zodiac*. An interesting contrast is provided by Giovanni Bellini's *Madonna and Child between St Catherine and the Magdalen* which reveals Bellini's typically Venetian sensitivity to colour and subtle modelling.

Room V Giorgione's *Tempest* is one of the most beautifully painted and tantalizing pictures in the world. There is no single correct interpretation of the story behind the woman feeding her baby and the soldier looking on but you can still feel the magic of this work. The picture of the *Old Woman* in the same room is painted as a warning, perhaps to the woman in *The Tempest*, of the ravages of time.

Another painting in this highly emotive room is the *Pietà*, painted around 1505 when Giovanni Bellini was an old man in his mid 70s. The warmth and compassion in this beautifully executed painting is echoed in a more gentle and tender way by the *Madonna with child and John the Baptist* which Bellini painted at about the same time.

Room VI In this room you come to paintings by Titian, who was a great exponent of the Venetian style of painting. He combined artistic sensibility with the kind of finish which made his paintings highly prized among his patrons. He used to apply as many as forty layers of glaze to achieve his effects. Also in this room you will find *Presentation of the Ring to Doge Bartolommeo Gradenigo* by Paris Bordone, a disciple of Titian and Giorgione.

Room VII Lorenzo Lotto, whose *Portrait of a Young Man* stands out in this room, worked mostly in the towns which Venice had conquered on the mainland. He was a follower of the Venetian school but also admired Botticelli, Raphael and the Florentine style.

Room VIII Palma il Vecchio is another of the painters who demonstrates the Venetian style at its best. His painting of the *Sacra Conversazione*, around 1525, may have had Titian's hand in it after Palma's death.

Room IX Here you can view some of the work of Palma's apprentice, Bonifacio de' Pitati. The painting of the *Eternal Father protecting Venice* shows the Piazza S. Marco as it was around 1530.

Room X Paolo Veronese was one of the grand style Venetian painters of the 16th century and his work was much in demand for the decoration of the Palazzo Ducale (Doge's Palace). *The Feast at the House of Levi* was originally painted in 1573 for the church of S.S. Giovanni e Paolo as a *Last Supper* but since the Inquisition objected to the introduction of dwarfs, dogs and Germans into the picture, Veronese decided to change its title rather than its content.

In **Room X** you can see paintings by the foremost painters of high Venetian style. Jacopo Tintoretto dazzles you with his virtuoso performance in creating *St Mark Freeing the Slave, St Mark Rescuing a Saracen* and the *Translation of the Body of St Mark*. With the Titian masterpiece, *Pietà*, these works show Venetian painting moving away from the delineation of subject and into a fluid use of colour and brush strokes which preceded the Impressionist movement.

Room XI Tintoretto's romantic, emotional style displayed in several of his paintings in this room contrasts well with the cool style of Veronese whose *Mystic Marriage of St Catherine* shows off his subtlety of colour. Room XI, while including the highest talents of the Venetian 16th century, also displays work by 17th-century followers who were mostly non-Venetians like Bernardo Strozzi and Luca Giordano — a Neapolitan renowned for his speed and dexterity with paint and nicknamed *Luca fa presto*.

There is also work here by Giambattista Tiepolo, an 18th century Venetian whose stylish paintings and frescoes were in great demand for palaces and churches in Italy, Spain and Germany. His paintings in this room include *The Miracle of the Bronze Serpent, St Helena Discovers the True Cross* and *The Faithful Worshippers* which he painted for the Scalzi church.

Rooms XII to XX These are of relatively less interest and if you are in a hurry you can skip them. Most of the works in these rooms were painted between the late 16th century and the 18th century by followers of the great Venetian masters.

Take time, however, to pause in **Room XVII** where, among the 18th-century views of Venice, you will find Canaletto's *Capriccio of a Colonnade Opening on a Courtyard* and several other views by Francesco Guardi. The *Island of San Giorgio* is a particularly good work. These paintings reveal that the patrons of painters were no longer Venetian institutions but the rich tourists who were now arriving to gaze upon the resplendent shell of what had once been the most important city in the world.

Rooms XX, XXI Here, we go back to the 15th and 16th centuries and view large, absorbing paintings which celebrated the patron saints of Venetian scuole in scenes set in Venice. The two leaders of this form of grand reportage were Vittorio Carpaccio and Gentile Bellini. The latter is represented, among other paintings, by the splendid *Corpus Domini Procession* in the Piazza S. Marco which is an excellent reproduction of the piazza as it was in 1496. Vittorio Carpaccio is represented by the *Recovery of a Man Possessed by Demons* which shows the old wooden Rialto bridge in 1496. Carpaccio is also well represented in Room XXI by perhaps his most well known series, the *St Ursula Cycle*, originally painted for the Scuola di Sant' Orsola which was attached to the church of S.S. Giovanni e Paolo. This cycle tells the story of St Ursula, daughter of the Christian king of Brittany who agreed to marry the son of the pagan king of England on condition that he became a Christian and would accompany her and her virgin attendants on a pilgrimage. The journey comes to a tragic end in Cologne when Julian, Prince of the Huns, massacres her and her attendants. The series ends with the martyrdom and funeral of St Ursula.

Rooms XXIII, XXIV The last two rooms of the Accademia are part of the original church and scuola of S. Maria della Carità and room XXIV contains the memorable Titian work, *Presentation of the Virgin* in its original position in the committee room of the scuola.   **7 H6** Vaporetto 1 or 2 to Accademia.

Museo Correr (Correr museum), Piazza S. Marco, S. Marco (tel: 25625). Opening times: 1000—1600, Sun 0930—1230. Closed Tues. This is the civic museum of Venice and it is located in the Procuratie Nuove which runs along the south side of the Piazza S. Marco. The collection was given to Venice by Teodoro Correr in 1830 and, after occupying the Fondaco dei Turchi, it was installed in the Procuratie Nuove in 1922.

The collection has grown since then and the museum is in three sections — the *Raccolte Storiche,* the *Risorgimento* and the *Quadreria.* You will find more detailed information in the museum but a few of the more outstanding features are drawn to your attention in this guide.

The entrance to the **raccolte storiche** (historical collection) is at the western end of the Piazza S. Marco near the monumental staircase by G.M. Soli and through the ballroom which was built in 1822. In the first rooms of the collection on the first floor, there are sculptures by Antonio Canova (1757—1822) whose sentimental style is expressed in *Daedalus and Icarus* and the earlier work, *Orpheus and Eurydice.*

There are well over 20 rooms in the historical collection, including a library. In the rooms, you will find exhibits of flags and other emblems of the lion of St Mark as well as clothing, letters and reports, objects of daily use, a coin collection, details of the construction and operation of Venetian ships and many other objects which describe the life of the Venetian Republic.

There are about 20 rooms in the **museo del risorgimento** section on the second floor which contain items relating to the period of Venetian history between the occupation by Napoleon and World War II but concentrating mainly on the freeing of Venice from Austrian domination. Unfortunately, you may be disappointed as these rooms are often closed.

The **Quadreria** (Picture gallery) on the second floor contains a mixed collection but there is special emphasis on Venetian painters and a visit here contributes significantly to your knowledge of the story of Venetian painting.

In **Rooms I and II** you will find some excellent 14th-century paintings. **Room III** has works by Lorenzo Veneziano and, in **Room IV**, the fresco technique, which was unusual in Venice, is ably performed by an unknown artist. **Room VI** has more advanced Gothic style paintings by Jacobello del Fiore and Michele Giambono. **Room VII** is devoted to the School of Ferrara, run by the Este family who were allies of Venice. The chief exponent of the Ferrara style is Cosmè Tura whose painting, *Pietà* in 1468, shows the sharp, brittle style of the school.

Rooms X and XI contain paintings by the Flemish artists who developed the technique of painting in oils and brought it to Venice. Antonello da Messina's *Dead Christ wih Angels* was painted in 1475 and is one of the earliest Italian oil paintings. This painting now hangs in room XI.

In **Room XIII** you will find works by the whole Bellini family. The *Crucifixion* was painted by Jacopo and the portrait of *Doge Giovanni Mocenigo* was painted by his son Gentile. Giovanni Bellini is represented by the *Transfiguration* which shows the influence of Mantegna.

From **Room XIV**, where there are works by Alvise Vivarini, you arrive in **Room XV** which has one of the most celebrated, but not necessarily one of the most interesting, paintings in the Quadreria. The painting, by Carpaccio, is of two women whom he calls *Courtesans* but they could easily be any two women of the period.

In **Room XVI,** there is another Carpaccio. A little further on, through more rooms containing a variety of paintings in the Byzantine tradition as well as a number of other interesting items, you will come to an impression of the famous Map of Venice made by Jacopo de' Barbari in 1500. It is said to be the most accurate map of its time.   **8** H5
Vaporetto 1, 2, 4 or 5 to S. Marco or S. Zaccaria.

Museo Fortuny (Fortuny Museum) Palazzo Pesaro degli Orfei, Campo S. Benedetto, S. Marco (tel: 700995). Opening times: 0830—1330. Closed Mon.

This collection was left by Mariano Fortuny, a Spaniard, born in 1876, who worked in Venice and became rich as a designer and manufacturer of pleated silk dresses. A few years after his death in 1949, his wife created the museum and it includes many of Fortuny's creations and paintings.   **7** J5
Vaporetto 1 to S. Angelo.

Galleria Giorgio Franchetti (Franchetti Gallery). Ca' d'Oro, Canal Grande, Cannaregio (tel: 52 38790). Opening times: 0900—1400, Sun 0900—1300. Closed Mon. This wonderful building, which was in a rather dilapidated state for many years, is now one of the most exciting museums in Venice as a result of the restoration work which was carried out by the generous Baron Franchetti. The museum resembles a luxurious house with excellent Venetian and Florentine paintings, sculptures, medallions and Renaissance bronzes tastefully exhibited in the refurbished interior. In particular, look out for the red Verona marble wellhead in the courtyard which was constructed in 1427 by Bartolommeo Bon. It was retrieved from antique dealers by Baron Franchetti and replaced in its original position. Mantegna's *S. Sebastian* is at the end of the portico and there are also important paintings by Bordone, Guardi, Titian and van Dyck. **4 J3**

Vaporetto 1 to station Ca' d'Oro.

Galleria Internazionale d'Arte Moderna and **Museo Orientale** (Gallery of Modern Art and Oriental Museum). Ca' Pesaro, Canal Grande, S. Croce. At the time of writing, these museums were temporarily closed but when they reopen, their hours are expected to be as below. Gallery of Modern Art (tel: 721127). Opening times: 0900—1600, Sun 0930—1230. Oriental Museum (tel: 27681). Opening times: 0900—1400, Sun 0900—1300. Both museums are closed Mon.

The Baroque palazzo was ordered in 1652 by Giovanni Pesaro who later became a Doge. It was begun by Longhena and finished by Antonio Gaspari who worked on the second floor and the façade facing Rio delle due Torri. The collection in the Gallery of Modern Art was founded in 1897 and consists mainly of works received from the exhibition at the Venice Biennale.

Browsing through the gallery is an interesting experience as it reflects 20th-century trends. Some of the most notable Italian works here are by Giacomo Manzù and Giorgio Mordani. There are also works by Kandinsky, Klee, Matisse and Rodin.

The Oriental Museum, on the top floor of the palazzo, is a miscellaneous collection of mostly Chinese and Japanese objects and works of art from the 10th to the 19th century. **4 J3**

Vaporetto 1 to S. Stae.

Raccoltà Peggy Guggenheim (Guggenheim Collection). Palazzo Venier dei Leoni, Canal Grande, Dorsoduro (tel: 706288). Opening times: 1400—1800 daily, April to October. Closed Tues. The Palazzo Venier was first built in 1749 by Lorenzo Boschetti but construction ceased after the ground floor was erected owing, it is said, to the opposition of the powerful Corner family who owned the palazzo across the canal. Whatever the

The Ca d'Oro, home of the Galleria Franchetti

reason, the Venier was not completed even by the millionaire heiress, Peggy Guggenheim, who installed her modern art collection in it. It is one of the biggest private collections in the world, and one of the best.

The collection includes paintings and sculptures by most of the leading artists of the 20th century and represents the major trends in modern art. Among the artists whose work you can view here are Arp, Chirico, Duchamp, Ernst, Giacometti, Magritte, Mondrian, Moore, Paolozzi, Picasso and Tanguy.

The Guggenheim collection is a memorial to an enlightened art collector and she is buried in the garden of the palazzo with her pet dogs.   **7** J6
Vaporetto 1 to Salute or lines 1, 2 or 4 to Accademia.

Pinacotèca Querini Stampalia (Querini Stampalia Picture Gallery). Palazzo Querini Stampalia. Campiello Querini, Castello (tel: 25235). Opening times: 1000—1545. Closed Mon. The 16th-century palazzo, which is near the church of S. Maria Formosa, was left to the city of Venice by Count Giovanni Querini in 1869. There is a library on the first floor and there are about 20 rooms in the second floor gallery which has an unlived-in, ghostly kind of atmosphere and contains an excellent collection of furniture, paintings, porcelain and other objects.

Room I You enter the gallery by this second floor room above the library. It contains a large collection of paintings by Gabriele Bella which provide an insight into life in Venice in the late 18th century. **Room II** contains a colourful painting of the *Coronation of the Virgin* by Caterino and Donato which was produced in the 1370s. In **Room III** there are portraits by Sebastiano Bombelli who was a fashionable painter of leaders of Venetian society in the 17th century. **Rooms IV to VII** contain minor Venetian works by artists such as Palma il Giovane and Schiavone and there are a number of genre scenes of the 17th century. **Room VIII** has several interesting Renaissance paintings including *The Presentation in the Temple* by the young Giovanni Bellini at the time when he was still greatly influenced by Mantegna. Experts believe that this painting is based on Mantegna's *Presentation*, a photographic reproduction of which hangs nearby. There are also two portraits by Palma il Vecchio which are of some interest as they portray Francesco Querini and his bride, Paola Priuli for whom he built this palazzo. The portrait of Paola Priuli is unfinished but the portrait of Francesco is in excellent condition. **Room IX** is one to pause in to admire the *Judith*

with the Holofernes by Vincenzo Catena who was a 15th/16th century Venetian following in the style of Giovanni Bellini and Cima.

Go straight through the short corridor which is **Room X** and on to **Room XI** which is a delightful room for lovers of the genre paintings by Pietro Longhi. On the walls, there hang Longhi paintings of the Sagredo family and the Michiel family. The painting of *Venetian Monks, Canons and Friars* depicts the religious men of 18th-century Venice whom Longhi saw as three distinct groups — those who live to enjoy themselves, those who study and those who pray. **Rooms XII and XIII** prolong the enjoyment of Longhi and Venetian life in the 18th century. **Rooms XV and XVI** complete the picture of Venetian life at the time with furnishings of the period.

The rest of the rooms in the gallery contain drawings, tapestries, furniture and some portraits of public servants and others. These rooms are relatively uninteresting and you may care to pass them by.   **5** L5
Vaporetto 1, 2, 4, or 5 to S. Zaccaria or 1, 2, or 4 to Rialto.

Museo del '700 Veneziano (Museum of 18th-century Venice) Ca' Rezzonico, Canal Grande, Dorsoduro (tel: 24543). Opening times: 1000—1800, Sun 0930—1230. Closed Fri. Longhena began to construct the Ca' Rezzonico, which is a large luxurious palazzo but, like the Pesaro, it was some time until it was finally completed in 1752 when Giorgio Massari finished the work for the Rezzonico family.

During the 19th century, poet Robert Browning lived here for some time and he died while staying in the Ca' Rezzonico in December 1889.

The Museum of 18th-century Venice was moved here in 1935 and consists of furniture, sculpture and paintings, including ceiling paintings brought in from other buildings.

You can reach the first *piano nobile* by a fine staircase built by Massari who also built the **ballroom**. The ceiling painting by Crosato is an important feature of this room and the vase stands are very elaborately sculpted. To the right lies the **Sala della Allegoria Nuziale** (Room of the Allegory of Marriage) which contains the Tiepolo allegorical ceiling painting of the Marriage of Ludovico Rezzonico to Faustina Sarvognan, a daughter of one of the powerful Venetian families.

The **Sala dei Pastelli** contains beautiful pastels by Rosalba Carriera. Carry on through to the **sala del Trono** (throne room) which, with its gilded throne by

Antonio Corradini and ceiling by G.B. Tiepolo, is one of the most spectacular rooms you will see.

The Sala del Tiepolo has an important ceiling painting by Tiepolo entitled *Fortitude and Wisdom* and the furniture in this room has been beautifully crafted by Andrea Brustolon. Beyond this room there is a library with 18th-century Venetian books. Passing through another room with paintings by Lazzarini, you will find the Sala del Brustolon which contains more excellent furnishings by Andrea Brustolon.

A staircase takes you up to the second floor where there are interesting 18th-century paintings including the *Death of Darius* by Piazzetta and *Judith and Holofernes* by Giovanni Liss.

Rooms of interest on the second floor include the **Sala delle Lacche Verdi**, a drawing room of green lacquer furniture which gives the room its name. The ceiling painting is by Gian Antonio Guardi and in the next room there are three exquisite Guardi frescoes. Beyond, there is a reconstructed 18th-century bedroom, the Camera dell' Alcova.

There are paintings by Giambattista Tiepolo's son, Giandomenico, who was a more down to earth and less allegorical artist. One of his most famous satirical paintings is *New World* which he painted in 1791 and it hangs here on the second floor.

The third floor is most interesting if you want to know about Venetian life styles in the 18th century. On display, there are Tiepolo drawings, a marionette theatre, an 18th-century pharmacist and Venetian dresser from the time. **7 G5**
Vaporetto 1 to Ca' Rezzonico.

Museo di Storia Naturale (Natural History Museum). Fondaco dei Turchi, Canal Grande, S. Croce (tel: 5235885). Opening times: 0900–1330, Sun 0900–1200. Closed Mon. The Fondaco dei Turchi was leased to Turkish merchants who traded with Venice from 1621–1838 and the original palace was rebuilt in 1869. You will find the Natural History Museum on the second floor.

Contents of the museum include fossils, underwater fauna and one of the largest skeletons of a dinosaur in the world.
Vaporetto 1 to S. Stae. **4 H3**

Piazza San Marco

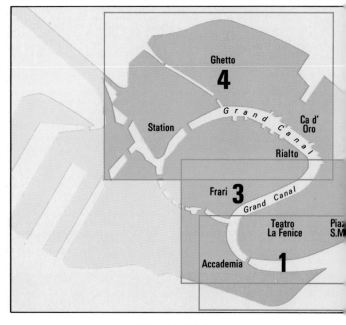

CITY WALKS

Walking in Venice is always a delight. Every time you visit, there is something new to discover — even on the most familiar routes: interesting architectural details, new viewpoints and street life is an ever-changing scene with visitors, tradesmen, business people, shoppers and children giving life to the calles and piazzas. As you walk along, you will find streets described in various ways:

Calle   street
Campiello   small square
Campo   square (literally a field. Originally, the campi were full of trees)
Corte   courtyard
Fondamenta   paving along a canal
Marzaria (Merceria) or *Ruga*   shopping street
Molo   quay
Piazza   the one and only Piazza S. Marco
Piscina   site of a pool
Ponte   bridge
Ramo   side street
Rio   any canal except Canal Grande, Cannaregio Canal and Giudecca Canal
Rio terrà   filled in canal
Riva   major fondamenta
Salizzada   the main streets of a parish

Sottoportico/Sottoportego   small street, either entered through an arch or covered.

The four routes outlined here are only suggestions as to how you can cover the six *sestieri* of Venice. There is no reason why you shouldn't make detours if you wish. Walking steadily, each route can be completed in less than half a day but the best way to enjoy the walks is to dawdle, lingering in the campos and taking time off to sit at cafés observing the scene which differs from one *sestiere* to another. In some parts of Venice, streets are so short and numerous that it would be impossible to go into detail without causing unnecessary confusion, especially as several places have more than one name! Spellings, too, can differ. For this reason, we have tried to keep the directions as simple as possible by omitting the names of some of the more complicated twists and turns but, if you follow the maps as you read, you should find the routes quite easy to follow.

Three of the walks include the Piazza S. Marco and this gives you an opportunity to visit just one or two of the big features of the piazza each time instead of trying to do them all in one day. See pp. 107–111.

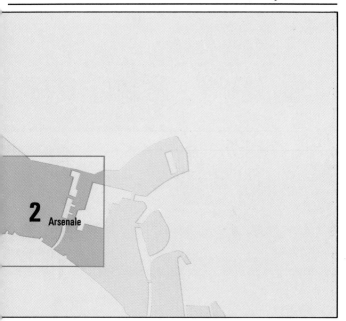

Walk One   S. Marco and Dorsoduro

This walk starts in the Piazza S. Marco and takes you through part of the sestieri of S. Marco and across the Canal Grande to Dorsoduro. You may visit the galleries of the Accademia and the Guggenheim Collection and the Museo Fortuny as well as the churches of S. Stefano and S. Maria della Salute. This walk also has many campos where you can stop and watch the world go by and enjoy a coffee or a snack.

Walk Two   S. Marco and Castello

In this walk you leave the Piazza S. Marco by the northeast corner, to the left of the Basilica, and you visit another part of the sestieri of S. Marco and almost all of the sestieri of Castello. Among the places you will see are the Museo Navale and the Arsenale where the Venetians built the ships that were used to dominate the Mediterranean. The churches on this walk include S. Zaccaria, S. Giovanni in Bragora and the great Gothic church of S.S. Giovanni e Paolo, known as Zanipolo.

Walk Three   S. Polo, Dorsoduro and S. Marco

This walk starts near the Rialto bridge and takes you through the sestieri of S. Polo as well as parts of Dorsoduro and back to S. Marco. You start in the centre of the market area and you may need to be generous with your time to allow yourself to enjoy this part of the walk. Other delights include the churches of S. Polo and S. Maria Glorioso dei Frari. Theatre lovers have the Museo Goldoni and the Teatro la Fenice, and you can pay another visit to the Accademia.

Walk Four   S. Marco and Cannaregio

This walk also starts near the Rialto bridge and takes you through other parts of the sestieri of S. Marco and on to the sestieri of Cannaregio. One of the high points of this walk is the Ca d'Oro which houses the Galleria Franchetti. There are several churches including the Madonna dell' Orto and the Scalzi. As well as the original Jewish Ghetto with its museum and synagogue, you may walk through a part of Venice seldom visited by tourists — where the typical life of Venice can be seen.

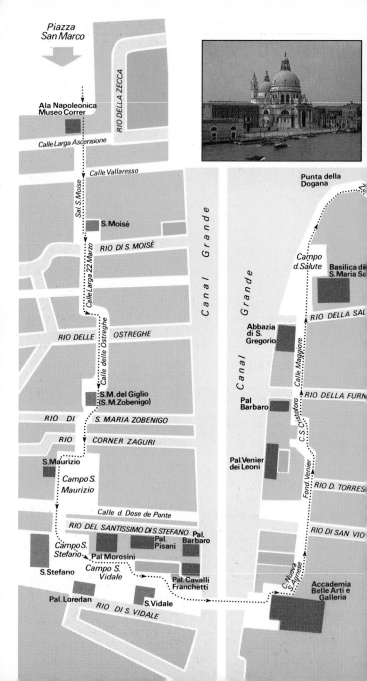

Piazza
San Marco

Ala Napoleonica
Museo Correr

RIO DELLA ZECCA

Calle Larga Ascensione

Calle Vallaresso

Sal. S. Moisè

S. Moisè

Canal Grande

RIO DI S. MOISÈ

Calle Larga 22 Marzo

Punta della
Dogana

Campo
d. Salute

Basilica di
S. Maria Sa

RIO DELLA SAL

RIO DELLE

OSTREGHE

Calle delle Ostreghe

Abbazia
di S.
Gregorio

Canal Grande

Canal Grande

Calle Maggiore

S.M. del Giglio
(S.M. Zobenigo)

RIO DI

S. MARIA ZOBENIGO

Pal.
Barbaro

RIO DELLA FURN

C. S. Cristoforo

RIO

CORNER ZAGURI

S. Maurizio

Campo S.
Maurizio

Pal. Venier
dei Leoni

Fond. Venier

RIO D. TORRES

Calle d. Dose de Ponte

RIO DEL SANTISSIMO DI S. STEFANO

Pal.
Pisani

Pal.
Barbaro

RIO DI SAN VIO

Campo S.
Stefano

Pal. Morosini

S. Stefano

Campo S.
Vidale

C. Nuova
S. Agnese

Pal. Loredan

S. Vidale

Pal. Cavalli
Franchetti

RIO DI S. VIDALE

Accademia
Belle Arti e
Galleria

Walk One   S. Marco and Dorsoduro

Leave the Piazza S. Marco by the southwest corner under the Ala Napoleonica. In Calle Larga Ascensione, there is a kiosk which sells foreign newspapers. Continue over the Calle Larga and through the arch. To the left, the Hotel Luna stands on the site of the inns where the Crusaders gathered before setting off for the Holy Land. Next on the left is the Calle Vallaresso which you might like to explore. It has some very smart shops and the famous Harry's Bar is at the far end near the S. Marco Vallaresso vaporetto stop. When you are ready to resume your route, continue walking along the Salizzada S. Moisè and you will soon come to the Campo S. Moisè which has a very ornate Baroque church (see p. 102). Ruskin had a very low opinion of this church but it is certainly more appealing than the stony modern face of the Bauer Grünwald hotel which is at right angles to it.

After crossing a bridge, you then walk along Calle Larga 22 Marzo (the date — 22 March — commemorates Doge Manin's revolt against the Austrians in 1848). There are several good hotels in this street including the Saturnia e International. **Palazzo Contarini Fasan**, popularly known as the 'House of Desdemona', and the famous de luxe hotels of the Canal Grande are to the left.

After the Calle Larga, you will pass through the Calle delle Ostreghe before arriving at another campo with an ornate church — **S.M. del Giglio** or **Zobenigo** (see p. 101). After two more bridges, you come to the large Campo S. Maurizio which has one of those wells with metal covers that feature quite often in Venetian campos. The church of **S. Maurizio** stands out to the north but the leaning campanile behind does not belong to it. The campanile belongs to the church of **S. Stefano** (see p. 103) which you can reach by taking a calle to the left of the church and crossing another bridge. Campo S. Stefano, often called Francesco Morosini on street maps, is very large and at its centre, there is a statue to a now largely forgotten 19th-century man of letters, Nicolò Tommaseo. There are two cafés at the entrance to the campo — good places for a grandstand view of life in the campo as you sip a leisurely drink. The palazzi **Loredan** and **Morosini** are in this campo and **S. Stefano**, a splendid building with a fine interior is on your right. If you have time, stop and look around the church.

If you would like to visit the **Palazzo Pisani** and **Palazzo Barbaro** (see p. 77), they are on the left side of the campo, when

Calle Larga 22 Marzo looking towards S. Moise

Campo S. Stefano (top), Palazzo Barbaro

you walk towards the canal. Crossing the campo from the church of S. Stefano, you pass the church of **S. Vidale** and arrive at the insensitively rebuilt **Palazzo Cavalli Franchetti** where cats are usually to be found sunning themselves against its walls.

As the wooden Accademia bridge before you may still be in the course of repair, cross by the temporary bridge to the **Accademia** where the best collection of paintings in Venice is housed in the former church of the Carità (see pp. 66-68). Many people find that they can best appreciate the Accademia by making several short visits rather than one long visit and this would be a good time to view at least some of the rooms. We pass the Accademia again in Walk Three.

Turn left at the Accademia along the Calle Nuova S. Agnese, signposted 'English Church'. There is usually a fish stall here, opposite a tiny restaurant. Carry straight on to the Campiello S. Vio, from which there is an excellent view of the Canal Grande. Then carry on through the Fondamenta Venier. Here the **Palazzo Venier dei Leoni** houses the **Raccoltà Guggenheim** (Guggenheim collection see pp. 69-70). Stop if you have time or return later for a most rewarding visit.

From the Palazzo Venier, continue through the Calle S. Cristoforo in the direction of the Canal Grande and on past the Palazzo Barbaro and Abbazia di S. Gregorio. This will bring you out to **S. Maria della Salute** and the Punta della Dogana from where there are wonderful views of the Lagoon. From the Punta della Dogana you can start walking down the Zattere, so called because wooden rafts (*zattere*) used to be moored here. There are still one or two left, some

with cafés built on them, giving you a good excuse to stop for a drink or a snack and enjoy the view across to the Giudecca and the Redentore church.

Some way along the Zattere, next to the attractive Campo di S. Agnese, you will come upon the huge **Gesuati church** (see p. 94). If you would like to see the *squero* where gondolas and other boats are built, make a detour off to the right and walk along the Fondamenta Nani. After this rewarding detour, carry on along the Zattere, until you reach the Calle Trevisan. If it is near lunch time you would do well at this point to cross the bridge over to the Rio delle Eremite and on to the Locanda Montin, which is in Fondamenta di Borgo. This is one of the most pleasant garden restaurants in Venice, much patronized by artists, writers and film people.

Proceed further along the Zattere until you come to Calle del Vento. Cross the Campo di S. Basegio and continue along the Fondamenta di S. Basilio until you come to a bridge. This will lead you directly to the church of **S. Sebastiano**

Gilding a gondola

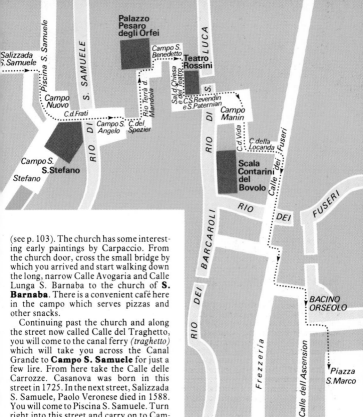

(see p. 103). The church has some interesting early paintings by Carpaccio. From the church door, cross the small bridge by which you arrived and start walking down the long, narrow Calle Avogaria and Calle Lunga S. Barnaba to the church of **S. Barnaba**. There is a convenient café here in the campo which serves pizzas and other snacks.

Continuing past the church and along the street now called Calle del Traghetto, you will come to the canal ferry *(traghetto)* which will take you across the Canal Grande to **Campo S. Samuele** for just a few lire. From here take the Calle delle Carrozze. Casanova was born in this street in 1725. In the next street, Salizzada S. Samuele, Paolo Veronese died in 1588. You will come to Piscina S. Samuele. Turn right into this street and carry on to Campiello Nuovo. The square links with the Calle dei Frati to the east of S. Stefano which you passed earlier in the walk. A few steps bring you to **Campo S. Angelo**, a handsome square with interesting palazzi. There is a plaque on the house in this square in which Cimarosa died in 1801.

Leaving the campo by the Calle del Spezier, signposted Rialto, turn left into the Rio Terrà della Mandola. You will come to the **Museo Fortuny** in the Palazzo Pesaro degli Orfei (see p. 68) and, if you have time, wander around the museum for a few minutes. The textiles and pleated dresses are particularly interesting. The main façade of the palazzo is on the small Campo S. Benedetto. From here, you now go down the Salizzada della Chiesa e del Teatro, past the Teatro Rossini and on to the Calle S. Revendin e S. Paternian. After a short distance, you will be in **Campo Manin**. The savings bank here stands on the site of the original print-

ing shop in which Aldus Manutius produced his fine editions. They are still admired today by printers and typographers as excellent and important examples of early printing. Some of his editions are on display in the Marciana library in the Piazzetta di S. Marco. The street on the right of Campo Manin will take you to **Contarini del Bovolo** which has a famous exterior spiral staircase.

From here, turn right out of the Calle della Locanda into Calle dei Fuseri. Shortly after crossing a bridge, turn left and then follow the Frezzeria to the right to Calle Zorzi. This brings you to Bacino Orseolo which is usually crowded with gondolas waiting for passengers from the hotels that surround it. The Piazza S. Marco lies through the portico by the buildings of the Procuratie Vecchie.

Walk Two   S. Marco and Castello

Leave Piazza S. Marco by the Piazzetta dei Leoncini, sometimes called Giovanni XXIII. There is always great activity here with children riding the porphyry lions, pigeons bathing in the piazzetta's fountain and people examining the Palace of the Bishops (Palazzo Patriarchale) and the church of S. Basso, which is sometimes used for exhibitions.

Continue along the narrow Calle di Canonica, which has several cafés, and on to the Rio di Palazzo o della Paglia. On the other side of the Rio, you will see the Palazzo Trevisan Capello which is now a glass showroom. From the bridge, if you look to your right, you can see the Ponte dei Sospiri (Bridge of Sighs) which joins the dungeons to the Doge's Palace (see p. 107). You now walk through Campo S. Filippo e Giacomo and Salizzada S. Provolo, passing cafés and restaurants on your way to **Campo S. Zaccaria**. Facing you is the beautiful Renaissance façade of the S. Zaccaria church. The interior is notable for its paintings including a marvellous *Virgin with Four Saints* by Giovanni Bellini.

From S. Zaccaria walk to your right down to the Riva degli Schiavone for a look at the excellent view across to S. Giorgio Maggiore. You may wish to enjoy a drink at one of the cafés which provide a grandstand view of the activity on the quayside. This is an area of large hotels, such as the de luxe Danieli, and various other categories of accommodation.

Walking eastwards, after crossing four bridges, you will find yourself in the Campo S. Biagio. If you are interested in ships, have a look at the **Museo Navale**. Turn left along Fondamenta dell' Arsenale and you will then be able to visit the famous **Arsenale** (see p. 105), so important in Venetian history. The Renaissance arch, statues of gods and the two sculptures of lions, have attracted visitors for centuries. The arch was the gateway to the Venetian powerhouse where ships were built to rule the Mediterranean. With the help of 16,000 craftsmen, a fighting craft could be built in a single day. Return along the Riva degli Schiavoni until you come to Calle del Dose (Doge). If you follow this calle, you will come to Campo Bandiera e Moro gia della Bragora. This campo commemorates two early heroes of the movement to unite Italy. Note the fine Gothic *pensione*, La Residenza, and the church of **S. Giovanni in Bragora** (see p. 98) which contains paintings by Cima da Conegliano and Alvise Vivarini. From here, take the Fondamenta dei Furlani to the **Scuola S. Giorgio degli Schiavone**, a small hall which was the meeting place for Dalmatian (Slav) seamen and inside, you can view some of Carpaccio's finest paintings.

Now cross the canal beside the scuola and go down the Calle del Lion to the Rio S. Lorenzo. From here there is a view of the leaning tower of the church of **S. Giorgio dei Greci**. Cross the Rio S. Lorenzo and turn right into the Fondamenta di S. Lorenzo which leads to Borgoloco S.

Fond di S.Lorenzo

Calle del Lion

Scuola S.Giorgio degli Schiavone

Fond. d.Furlani

Arsenale

Sal. S. Antonin

RIO DEI GRECI

S.Giorgio dei Greci

RIO DELLA PIETA

Campo Bandiera e Moro gia d.Bragora

Calle del Dose

S.Giovanni in Bragora

RIO CA DI DIO

RIO DELL'ARSENALE

Fond. dell'Arsenale

Museo Navale

Campo S. Biagio

Riva degli Schiavoni

S. Marco

Medieval lions guard the Arsenale

Lorenze. When you reach Fondamenta di S. Severo, cross the first bridge you come to which will lead you past the Palazzo Grimani to the Ruga Giuffa.

Turn right into the extensive **Campo di S. Maria Formosa**. The church tower has a horrific face which Ruskin particularly disliked. At the southern side, over a bridge, the **Palazzo Querini Stampalia** has a fine library and a collection of 18th-century paintings and furniture in rooms with a ghostly kind of atmosphere (see p. 70).

Leave the campo by its eastern exit along Calle Lunga S. Maria Formosa and, turning off at Calle dell' Ospedale, you will come to Salizzada S.S. Giovanni e Paolo where there is a most extreme example of a Baroque façade on the church of S. Maria dei Derelitti, more commonly known as **Ospedaletto**.

The **Campo dei S.S. Giovanni e Paolo** is just a few steps away. It is notable for its great Gothic church (see p. 98) which contains many tombs of Doges. If

S.S. Giovanni e Paolo and the Colleoni Statue, (opposite) San Zaccaria

time is short just now, it's worth coming back later to look around the interior. Verrocchio's marvellous equestrian statue of Bartolommeo Colleoni stands on the west side of the campo. Colleoni was a Venetian mercenary commander who, upon his death, left money for the statue to be erected in the Piazza S. Marco. After some difficulties in completing the statue, it was finally placed here in Campo S.S. Giovanni e Paolo which the Venetians decided was just as good a spot for it.

Beside the west end of the church, you can find the **Scuola di S. Marco**, a splendid Renaissance building which is now a hospital but, usually, you can have a look around if you ask at the door.

Cross the bridge from this side of the campo and walk down the Calle Larga Giacinto Gallina. After three more bridges, you will come to Pietro Lombardi's 'jewel casket' church of the **Miracoli** which has walls covered with marble both inside and out. This is a beautiful and much admired building and you will probably want to linger at it for a while.

From the Miracoli, follow the Calle Castelli and the Fondamenta Sanùdo to Campo di S. Marina. Continue along the Calle del Dose (Doge) and the Calle del Pistor. Cross the bridge and then walk straight on until you come to the church of S. Lio which is named after Pope Leo X (1513–1521).

From here the Calle della Fava will bring you to the campo of the same name. The 18th-century church, here, houses some excellent paintings by G. B. Tiepolo and G. B. Piazzetta. Cross the bridge and walk along the Calle dei Stagneri. Turn left into the Merceria 2 Aprile. You will now find yourself at the side entrance of the huge church of **S. Salvatore** (see p. 103). There are some excellent paintings by Titian to be viewed inside but if you have had enough of churches for one morning you may prefer to saunter down the Merceria S. Salvatore and window shop in the smart boutiques all the way to Piazza S. Marco.

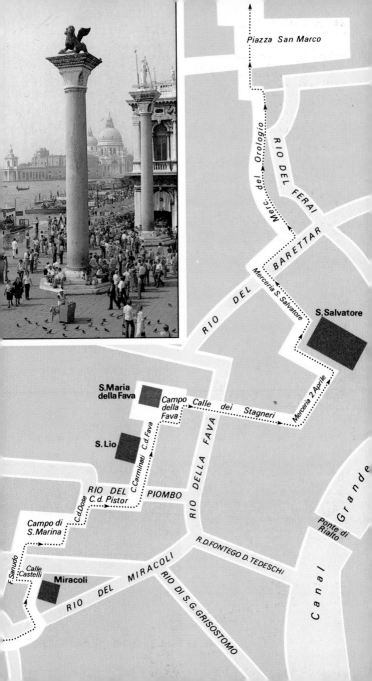

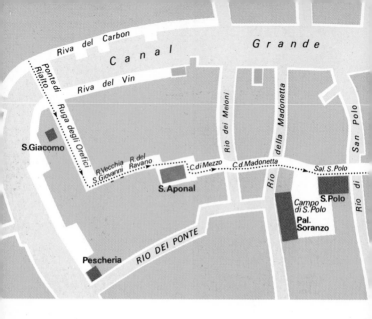

Walk Three S. Polo, Dorsoduro and S. Marco

This walk begins in the Rialto area on the bank of the Canal Grande. As you head for the Ponte di Rialto (Rialto bridge), you will find that this is an excellent area for buying holiday souvenirs or presents. There are leather bags, scarves and other tourist bric-a-brac, all at good prices. The Ruga degli Orefici, which is on the S. Polo side of the Ponte di Rialto, is crowded with market stalls. Make time to experience the Venetian market atmosphere as you stroll around the fruit and vegetable markets and along the Canal Grande to the Pescheria which sells an enormous variety of fish.

The church to the right is **S. Giacomo** which is commonly known as Giacometto (see p. 97) and, across the piazza in front of the church, you will see the **Gobbo**. This is a hunchback figure of stone from which proclamations were read out when Venice ruled the Republic. This figure was one end of the gauntlet that miscreants were obliged to run for some crimes. The other end is in the Piazza S. Marco.

All around this area, the streets are

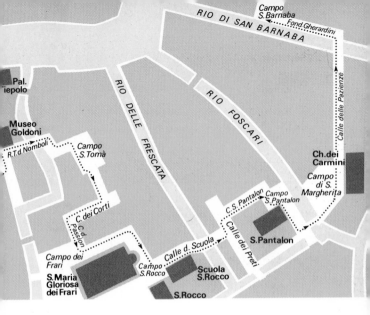

filled with lively, noisy crowds and there is a great temptation to linger for cream buns and coffee at one of the cafés.

When you are ready, leave the Ruga degli Orefici and turn left into the Ruga Vecchia S. Giovanni. Carry straight on through Rughetta del Ravano and you will soon arrive at **Campo S. Aponal** where the church has a rather fine façade. You may not be able to enter the church as its interior is being worked upon. Leave by the Calle di Mezzo and walk straight on. Treat yourself to a warm cinnamon bun at the baker on the right in Calle della Madonetta. You will soon arrive at the **Campo di S. Polo** which is the second largest square in Venice with its handsome palazzi. The Soranzo and Tiepolo are just behind you on the same side as the café at which you may wish to stop and enjoy the scene over a cup of coffee. In the rather dim interior of the church of S. Polo you will find works by G. B. Tiepolo, Tintoretto and Veronese. The church campanile, which has two Romanesque lions at its base, is separated from the church by the Salizzada S. Polo. Walk along the saliz-

zada and straight on to the Rio Terrà dei Nomboli. The **Museo Goldoni** is at the end of the rio terrà. This little theatre museum is worth visiting for a few minutes if it's open. Continue past the Museo Goldoni in a direction away from Campo di S. Polo and you will come to Campo S. Tomà. Leave the campo by the west side and turn right into Calle dei Corti. Take the third turning on the left and you will find yourself in the Campo dei Frari beside the vast Franciscan church of **S. Maria Gloriosa dei Frari** (see p. 94) which was built as a 'sister' church of S.S. Giovanni e Paolo. Both are excellent Gothic buildings and most people regard them as being two of the most outstanding churches in Venice. The Frari contains many superb sculptures and paintings including Titian's *Assumption* which is over the altar, the marvellous *St John the Baptist* by Donatello in one of the south choir chapels and a memorable Giovanni Bellini work in the sacristy.

In a small campo at the apse end of the Frari, you will find the church of S. Rocco next to the Scuola Grande di S. Rocco.

The clockface of S. Giacomo

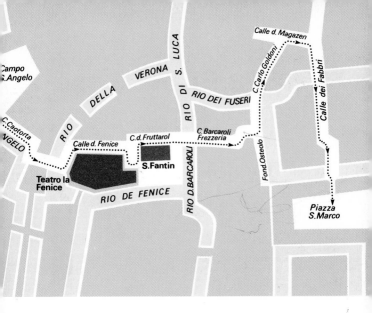

The scuola is home of a world-renowned series of paintings by Tintoretto including a very powerful *Crucifixion*.

From the Frari, take the Calle della Scuola. Make a left turn into Calle dei Preti and then right into Calle S. Pantaleone and its campo. The church (see p. 103), here, has an extraordinary trompe l'oeil ceiling. Crossing the Rio Foscari, you arrive at Campo di S. Margherita. This is a long campo with a shop and a clump of trees at its centre and the **Carmini** church (S. Maria del Carmelo) is at the southern end. The interior of the church is richly decorated and there are some excellent paintings.

Leave the campo S. Margherita by its southwest corner and, after crossing a bridge, turn left from Calle delle Pazienze into Fondamenta Gherardini. Leave the Campo S. Barnaba by the southern exit along Calle del Lotto and Calle della Toletta. Cross the bridge to Fondamenta Nani and turn left, then right into Calle del Pistor which leads you to the **Accademia** (see p. 66). These galleries are a must for any visitor to Venice and even if you had a

look around while following Walk One, you may agree that the galleries are well worth another visit.

When you are ready, cross the bridge and walk straight through Campo S. Vidal and Campo S. Stefano which you also visited in Walk One. Continue through Calle dei Frati and turn right along the south side of Campo S. Angelo and then along the Calle Caotorta. This calle leads across a bridge to the **Teatro la Fenice** (see p. 114). In front of the theatre, you can see the church of **S. Fantin** and the restaurant Al Teatro where you will experience a jolly atmosphere and a variety of services from pizzeria to full restaurant.

From here, take the Calle del Fruttarol over the narrow bridge to the Calle Barcaroli Frezzeria. Continue left across a bridge to the Calle Carlo Goldoni. Then turn right into the Calle del Magazen and right again into Calle del Fabbri. On the way along this calle, you pass the excellent Noemi restaurant. If you're not hungry at the moment, remember it for a later occasion and, when you're ready, carry on along Calle del Fabbri to Piazza S. Marco.

Walk Four S. Marco and Cannaregio

This walk begins at the **Campo S. Bartolommeo** near the Ponte di Rialto. The statue of Carlo Goldoni looks down from his pedestal at the crowds in this busy centre of Venice. Beyond the campo, continue north on the Salizzada S. Giovanni Grisostomo (signposted Ferrovia) to the church of S. Giovanni Grisostomo (see p. 98) which is on your right. Inside, you will find excellent paintings by Giovanni Bellini and Sebastiano del Piombo.

The walk continues through the campo and over a bridge. Turn left and carry on over another bridge until you come to a large campo and the church of **S.S. Apostoli** which has some interesting paintings inside. Busy cafés in the campo are filled mainly with Venetians rather than with tourists because many working people live in this area. The Strada Nova, which is a broad street to the left, goes towards the railway station. There are small shops and cafés and often a fish stall which is a common feature of this area.

The Calle della Ca' d'Oro to the left of the Strada Nova leads to the **Ca' d'Oro** (see p. 68). This beautiful building, which houses the **Galleria G. Franchetti**, is well worth a visit either now or later when you have more time. A little further on along the Strada Nova, you can see the tree-filled garden of the **Palazzo Giovanelli** on the right where statuary from villas and churches is on sale. You will shortly arrive at the Campo S. Fosca. Cross the Rio della Maddalena and, on your left, you will see the round neoclassical Maddalena church.

Following the Rio Terrà della Maddalena, the next bridge over Rio S. Marcuola brings you to the Campiello dell' Anconetta. Turn right here along Calle dell' Aseo which will bring you to the Rio della Misericordia. This is a long canal, stretching from northwest to southeast across Cannaregio, and bordered mostly by ordinary working people's houses. The canal is filled with boats transporting produce or engaged on other business errands.

The statue of Carlo Goldoni

Grande

Rio Terrà Lista di Spagna

Campo S. Geremia

Ponte Guglie

Campiello dell' Anconetta

Rio Terra San Leonarda

Calle dell' Aseo

Canale di Cannaregio

RIO DI GHETTO NUOVO

Ghetto Vecchio

Campo del Ghetto Nuovo

MISERICORDA

Ormesini

RIO DELLA SENSA

della Sensa

DELL' ORTO

donna dell'Orto

Turn left along the Fondamenta degli Ormesini and then right at the second opening you come to, called Calle del Forno. Cross the Rio della Sensa where there is a small, unpretentious café by the canal on the right. Continue along the Calle Loredan which is slightly to the left. From here, you cross at the Rio della Madonna dell' Orto. Turn right and you will arrive at the campo and church of **Madonna del Orto** (see p. 95). This is one of Venice's most important churches and you should, if possible, take time to look around the church. Tintoretto was buried here and many of his works are on view.

From the Madonna del Orto retrace your steps to the Rio della Misericordia and turn right along the Fondamenta degli Ormesini until you come to a pretty cast iron bridge. It's the third one along. This will lead you into the **Campo del Ghetto Nuovo**, which is, in fact, the older part of the Ghetto. This campo, in which the **Museo Israelitico** is situated, is the centre of the area where most of the Jewish community once lived. (See p. 107.)

Leave the campo by the Ghetto Vecchio and turn left for the Ponte Guglie. The scene here is always busy with a fish stall and other market activities. The Ponte Guglie is on the main route to the Ferrovia (railway station) and leads into **Campo S. Geremia**. The campo has a large church and some small cafés along its north side. Leave by the Rio Terrà Lista di Spagna — a wide street bordered by attractive houses which have become inexpensive hotels or bars of the kind usually found around stations. At the end of the Rio Terrà Lista di Spagna, you will find the **Scalzi church** (see p. 104), built for the barefoot order of Carmelites. The Roma hotel and restaurant is opposite. This popular hotel has a terrace overlooking the Canal Grande and a welcome stop if you are feeling tired. From the Scalzi bridge beside the hotel, you can take a vaporetto all the way down the Canal Grande unless you feel sufficiently restored to walk back via the *sestieres* of S. Croce and S. Polo to the Accademia bridge.

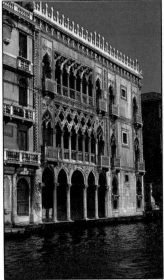

The Ca d'Oro

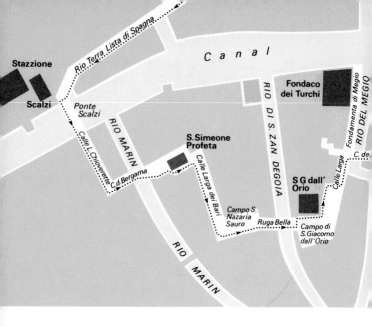

This part of the walk from Ferrovia to the Accademia is interesting, not so much for its monuments but because it crosses an area rarely visited by tourists and you have the opportunity to see more typical aspects of the Venetian way of life.

From the Scalzi bridge, walk straight on along Calle Lunga Chioverette. Turn left along the Calle della Bergama over the Rio Marin. Across the bridge, you will find the church of **S. Simeone Profeta** (also known as S. Simeone Grande) which possesses some fine paintings by artists such as Tintoretto. Take the Calle Larga dei Bari which is behind the church to the right. This leads to Campo S. Nazario Sauro and, if you follow the Ruga Bella, you will arrive at the Campo di S. Giacomo dall'Orio which has a fine church (rebuilt in the 13th century) with some excellent Veronese paintings and an unusual 14th-century ship's-keel roof.

From the northeast of the campo, take the Calle Larga to the junction with Calle Spezier and cross the bridge to the right. (The Fondamenta di Megio, in the oppo-

site direction, leads to the Fondaco dei Turchi natural history museum). Continue along the Calle del Tintor to the Salizzada S. Staè on the left which brings you to the Canal Grande. Here, you will find the **S. Staè** church which has an interesting Baroque façade and 18th-century paintings in the interior. An iron bridge from the campo leads to Calle Pesaro and the Ca' Pesaro Museum of Modern Art and Oriental Museum (see p. 69). When you're ready to move on, follow the fondamenta until you reach a calle to the left and then to the right. You will shortly arrive at the campo and the restored church of **S. Maria Mater Domini**. Then walk over the bridge and left, passing the Palazzo Gozzi. Turn right into the Campo S. Cassiano where the church has several excellent works by Tintoretto.

From here the Calle del Cristi leads to the Calle dei Botteri where you turn right towards the arcaded Pescheria (fish market), the Erberia (fruit and vegetable market) and the Ponte di Rialto.

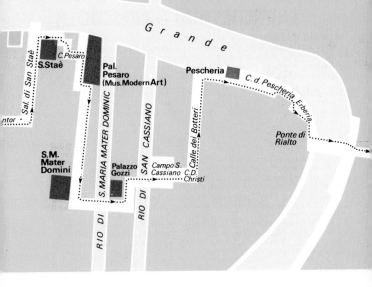

G r a n d e

Sal. di San Staè

S.Staè

C. Pesaro

Pal. Pesaro
(Mus. Modern Art)

Pescheria

C. d. Pescheria E. berìa

S.M. Mater Domini

RIO DI S. MARIA MATER DOMINIC

Palazzo Gozzi

RIO DI SAN CASSIANO

Campo S. Cassiano

C.D. Christi

Calle dei Botteri

Ponte di Rialto

ntor

Palazzo Barbarigo

CHURCHES AND THEIR SCUOLA

Angelo Raffaele   6 E6
Campo dell'Angelo Raffaele, Dorsoduro.
A 17th-century church which contains an
interesting series of paintings by Gian-
antonio Guardi telling the *Story of Tobias*.

Carmini   6 F5
Campo dei Carmini, Dorsoduro. Also
known as S. Maria del Carmelo, this 17th-
century church, which was originally
founded in the 14th century, has a distinctive campanile with a large statue of the
Virgin at the top. In the dark interior of the
church there are paintings on the arcades
of the nave which illustrate the history of
the Carmelite order. Paintings above the
altars include the Cima di Conegliano
work *Adoration of the Shepherds* and a Lorenzo Lotto *St Nicholas Bari with St John
the Baptist and St Lucy.*
  Also in the campo, the Carmelite Scuola
is well worth a visit to see the ceiling on the
first floor by G B Tiepolo in one of the
splendidly decorated rooms.

Frari   4 G4/5
Campo dei Frari, S. Polo. The Franciscan
church of S. Maria Gloriosa dei Frari is
one of the great churches of Venice
although its red brick simplicity comes as
something of a surprise to eyes accus-
tomed to northern Gothic architecture.
  The huge building resembles its sister
church, the Dominican S.S. Giovanni e
Paolo (S. Zanipolo) across the Canal
Grande. By the time it was consecrated in
1492, the Frari was drawing as large con-
gregations as S. Zanipolo.
  The façade of the church, though large,
is hardly more impressive than an enormous Victorian railway shed although its
campanile and one or two decorations,
which are dwarfed by the large area of
brick wall, are noteworthy features. Over
the south door there is an attractive
Madonna and child carving and over the
front portal, there is a *Risen Christ* by
Alessandro Vittoria whose works can be
examined at the Franchetti gallery.
  When you first enter the church, one of
the first things you notice is how clear and
almost unfurnished the building looks in
contrast to S. Marco's enclosed, heavily
ornamented atmosphere. The design of
the interior naturally draws the visitor to
the altar, over which the Titian *Assumption* hangs. If you enter the church from
the southeast, the Titian work is viewed
through the monks choir which stands like
a redoubt between you and the chancel — a
perhaps unintentional but, nevertheless,
effective device. Monuments to Doge

Francesco Fóscari and Doge Nicolò Tron
on each wall are very highly regarded. To
each side of the high altar, there are
chapels with works by Bartolommeo Vivarini and Mario Basati and, in the corner
chapel, there is a fine font statuette of *St
John the Baptist* by Sansovino. A superb
full size *St John the Baptist* by Donatello is
in the Florentine chapel by the chancel.
  On the left wall of the church, the *Monument to Canova*, with its stone figures
standing at the dark open door of a pyr-
amid is a melodramatic piece of kitsch that
works and you may find yourself, like the
stone figures, waiting in suspense. The
tomb was conceived by Canova as a monument for Titian.
  Next to the Canova monument, the Pesaro monument frames the side door. It is a
heavy and elaborate work but it has a
rough Baroque charm. The lovely Titian
work, *Virgin and Child*, which is nearby is
an important painting in Venetian artistic
history. For the first time, the figures
appear symmetrically, harmonising with
one another. The Titian work is a superb
example of the master's craftsmanship
only rivalled by his spectacular altarpiece.
Both works show Titian's preference for
using as many as forty layers of glaze.
  In the right transept of the church, you
will find the Beato Pacifico monument
which is elaborately decorated. The transept leads to the Sacristy where another
wonderful surprise awaits you. This is the
Giovanni Bellini *Madonna and child with
Saints Nicholas, Peter, Mark and Benedict*,
one of the true Venetian masterpieces.
  Behind the apse of the Frari lies the
16th-century *Scuola Grande di S. Rocco*
next to the church of S. Rocco. The Scuola
houses a remarkably fine series of Tintoretto paintings which include a magnificent *Crucifixion* and other dramatic scenes
from the New Testament painted with the
passionate intensity which characterizes
Tintoretto's best work.

Gesuati   7 G6
Fondamenta delle Zattere, Dorsoduro.
S. Maria del Rosario was built for the
Jesuits *(Gesuati)* and is now commonly
known as the Gesuati. The Jesuit church
was taken over by the Dominicans when
the Gesuati were suppressed for their dis-
orderly conduct. The large Rococo church
was built by Massari, who borrowed the
design from the Redentore church across
the Giudecca Canal. He gave the interior a
lighter Rococo spirit which is enhanced by
the light touch of Tiepolo's work on the
ceiling frescoes.

Gesuiti   5 L3

Campo dei Gesuiti, Cannaregio. An over-done Baroque church by Domenico Rossi who was commissioned to construct it in 1715 after the Venetians overcame their suspicions about the Jesuit order. One reason for visiting this church is the Titian *Martyrdom of St Lawrence.* This was Titian's first successful attempt at painting a night scene but it has suffered some damage over the centuries.

Madonna dell'Orto   2 J2

Campo Madonna dell'Orto, Cannaregio. This charming Venetian Gothic church was restored by the British Italian Art and Archives Fund. The elegant brick façade is decorated with white stonework. Originally called S. Cristoforo, the church was renamed Madonna dell'Orto when a miraculous image of the Virgin was found in the garden *(orto).* The well-proportioned interior has some superb paintings by Tintoretto such as *The Adoration of the Golden Calf* and the *Last Judgment* which hang in the chancel. Excellent paintings by Cima di Conegliano, Giovanni Bellini and others complete this visual display.

Miracoli   5 L4

Campo dei Miracoli, Cannaregio. S. Maria dei Miracoli is a beautifully finished church by Pietro Lombardo. Many kinds of marble cover the exterior and interior walls and little statues by Lombardo's son, Tullio, decorate the interior.

Ospedaletto   5 L4

Salizzada S.S. Giovanni e Paolo, Castello.

S. Maria dei Derelitti (waifs), known as Ospedaletto, has an extravagant Baroque façade which seems quite inappropriate for the narrow street from which it was designed to be viewed. The interior of the church contains typically 17th–18th century work by Palma il Giovane and others as well as an early Tiepolo.

Pietà   8 M5

Riva degli Schiavoni, Castello. Massari's church, S. Maria della Pietà, faces the lagoon. One of G. B. Tiepolo's airy ceiling frescoes, *the Triumph of Faith,* can be viewed from the elegant oval body of the church. Some of Vivaldi's best compositions were written for the institute behind the church where the orphan girls lived and they sang his music in the two choirs of the church.

Redentore   12 J8

Campo Redentore, Giudecca. This church, which was designed by Palladio in 1577 was, like the Salute, built as an expression of thankfulness that the plague had come to an end. It was completed by da Ponte, architect of the Rialto Bridge. The exterior, which is typical of Palladio, has a superimposed temple façade. The interior, on a Latin cross plan, has a classical form, giving the impression of strength and tranquillity. The light streams in through the vaulted ceiling in characteristic Palladio manner. Paintings in the church are mainly by followers of Tintoretto, Veronese, Bellini and Cima but there are originals by Alvise Vivarini, Bassano and Palma il Giovane.

Il Redentore, on La Guidecca

S. Georgio Maggiore

On the *Festa del Redentore* (the third Sunday in July), a bridge of boats is built from Dorsoduro to the church. There is also a dramatic firework display which lights up the night sky.

S.S. Apostoli   4 K4

Campo S.S. Apostoli, Cannaregio. The tall 17th-century campanile is the main exterior feature of this church. In the spacious interior you will find the late 15th-century Chapel of the Corner Family. *The Communion of St Lucy* hangs over the altar. There is an interesting marble head of St Sebastian by Tullio Lombardo in the chapel to the right of the high altar.

S. Bartolommeo   4 K4

Campo S. Bartolommeo, S. Marco. Although it was founded in the 9th century, this church was rebuilt many times between then and the 18th century and is, at present, in the process of restoration. Paintings inside include the *Martyrdom of S. Bartolommeo* by Palma il Giovane and organ doors by Sebastiano del Piombo but you are unlikely to be given the opportunity to enter the church.

S. Francesco della Vigna   5 N4

Campo della Fraternita, Castello. Vineyards once surrounded this Palladio

church at the northeastern corner of Venice. The outstanding feature of the church is its tall campanile which is sometimes mistaken for that of the Piazza S. Marco when seen from the lagoon. The interior of the church contains two interesting bronzes by Alessandro Vittoria. Carvings by Lombardo and his followers are in the Giustiani chapel.

S. Giacomo dall'Orio   4 H4

Campo S. Giacomo dall'Orio, S. Croce. This old church was founded in the 9th century and, although altered later, it retains an old world atmosphere with its ship's-keel roof. Among the stone columns of the nave and transept, there are two which were brought back to Venice with the other spoils of war after the sacking of Byzantium during the Fourth Crusade.

S. Giacomo di Rialto   4 K4

Campo S. Giacomo, S. Polo. S. Giacometto, as it is popularly called, is the oldest church in Venice. Construction began in the early 5th century but it was rebuilt in the 12th century. The façade is charming with its huge clock and Gothic portico. The interior is mainly Byzantine except for the large Baroque altarpieces which the church could well do without. In the main chapel, there is a statue of St James by Alessandro Vittoria. The nave altars reveal the relationship between the church with the market businesses outside — one is the altar of the grain winnowers *(garbeladori)* and the other is the altar of the goldsmiths *(orefici)*.

S. Giobbe   1 F2

Campo S. Giobbe, Cannaregio. Although construction first began under the instructions of Antonio Gambello in the 1450s, it was not completed until Pietro Lombardo enlarged it several decades later. The façade shows evidence of Tuscan Renaissance influence and has a portal showing S. Bernardino, whose visit to Venice inspired the building of the church. The interior has a domed chancel and three exquisitely-decorated chapels. Some of the most interesting paintings include *Nativity* by Gerolamo Savoldo and the *Annunciation* by Antonio Vivarini. The Martini chapel was built for a family of silk weavers from Lucca and it contains pretty medallions from the della Robbia workshop.

S. Giorgio dei Greci   8 M5

Calle dei Greci, Castello. The exterior is distinguished by its pretty campanile which leans perilously over towards the Rio dei Greci. The Greek orthodox community still worship at this church which was built in the 16th century and designed by Lombardo for Greek merchants. The interior has a late-Byzantine atmosphere, displaying Byzantine paintings and icons. There is a museum in the Scuola di S. Nicolò dei Greci nearby where you can see an interesting collection of icons.

S. Giorgio Maggiore   13 M7

Isola S. Giorgio Maggiore. Palladio's S. Giorgio Maggiore is a landmark of the Venetian lagoon with its tall campanile and it has appeared in countless paintings. The interior is as impressive as the outside. The absence of intricate decoration gives the interior a remarkable serenity, lit by shafts of sunlight which enter through the windows of the vaulting in true Palladio manner.

You enter the chancel between a pair of candelabra by Nicolò Roccatagliata. Over the high altar you will see a bronze group of figures by Gerolamo Campagna and two fine works by Tintoretto, the *Last Supper* and the *Fall of Manna*. In the choir, there are two interesting bronze statues by Roccatagliata.

In the right hand aisle, there are various works by Bassano and Tintoretto. In the left aisle, there is a sculptural group showing the *Virgin and Child* by Gerolamo Campagna and a Bassano painting of *St Lucy*.

In the Chapel of the Dead there is a painting over the altar of the *Deposition* which is attributed to Tintoretto. When he painted this important work, he was over 80 years of age and a dying man.

Behind the church you will see the **Giorgio Cini Cultural Foundation** which was previously a monastery. Now the Cultural Foundation is open on special occasions for exhibitions or you can ask to look around if the building is not being used for another purpose. The Foundation is housed in buildings by Palladio, Longhena and Buora. In the gardens there are occasional performances at the open-air theatre, Teatro Verde.

S. Giovanni in Bragora 8 M5

Campo Bandiera e Moro, Castello. This small Gothic church contains three important paintings: the triptych *Virgin and Child between St John the Baptist and St Andrew* by Bartolommeo Vivarini, a *Resurrection* by Alvise Vivarini and a *Baptism of Christ* by Cima da Conegliano.

S. Giovanni Grisostomo   5 K4

Campo S. Giovanni Grisostomo. Cannaregio. Mauro Codussi completed this terra cotta coloured church the year he died (1504). It is built on a simple Greek-cross structure and its open-plan centre with the central dome is spacious and uncluttered. Over the high altar there is a fine painting of *S. Giovanni Grisostomo and Saints John the Baptist, Liberale, Mary Magdalene, Agnes and Catherine* by Sebastiano del Piombo. Over an altar in the right-hand aisle, there is a Giovanni Bellini painting of *St Jerome, St Christopher and St Augustine,* one of the great artist's last works. Over the altar on the left is a carving by Tullio Lombardo of the *Coronation of the Virgin among the Apostles.*

S.S. Giovanni e Paolo   5 L4

Campo dei S.S. Giovanni e Paolo, Castello. This great Dominican church is also known as S. Zanipolo (a contraction of the two saints' names in local dialect). Many doges and other leading figures in Venetian history were buried here. This church not only has a beautiful interior but you can also learn a great deal about Venetian history as you look around it.

Like the Frari, which was built around the same time, the exterior of the church is not particularly interesting but there are many fine features in its interior. The Frari and S.S. Giovanni e Paolo have several features in common but they are sufficiently different for each visitor to be able to form an opinion as to which one he prefers. The choice is entirely personal.

Entering by Gambello's 15th-century portal on the west side, you come into the spacious church and it is this spaciousness which first strikes you as an important feature of the interior design.

As you wander around, you will see the monuments to the doges and excellent paintings such as the Bellini work, *St Vincent Ferrer with Sts Christopher and Sebastian* and the rare ceiling painting *Episodes from the life of St Dominic* which is in the chapel of S. Domenico. In the right transept you will find an Alvise Vivarini painting of *Christ bearing the Cross* and a Lotto painting of *St Antonio giving alms*.

The apse of the church has an imposing chancel with two flanking chapels. The high altar in Baroque style is probably by Longhena and on the walls of the chancel, there are tombs of Doges Michele Morosoni and Leonardo Loredano. On the left, there is a very highly regarded monument to Andrea Vendramin by Pietro Lombardo with carvings by Pietro's son, Tullio. Next to it there is an unfinished monument to Doge Marco Corner and statues of the Madonna and child by Nino Pisano.

The most interesting of the chapels is the one on the right with a sculptural group showing the *Virgin and St John* by Alessandro Vittoria. There is also a monument to Sir Edward Windsor, an English Earl who died in 1574.

S. Marco   8 K5

Piazza S. Marco, S. Marco. The Basilica of S. Marco was built to house the body of St Mark which was smuggled out of Egypt and into Venice in 828. The church was then a small private doge's chapel but in the 15th century it was enlarged and remodelled, the domes were heightened and Gothic spires and decorations were added. During this period, the interior of the church was enriched by the spoils of war against the Saracens in the east and the Venetians returned with many valuable items following the sacking of the city of Constantinople. The Basilica also benefited from the growing contributions of Italian artists whose knowledge and techniques were constantly improving.

Unlike many Venetian churches, the Basilica is as satisfying to the eye from the outside as it is from inside. From the Piazza, visitors enjoy simply standing and admiring the curved portals, the gold mosaics of which glitter in the sunlight, and the curvilinear upper storey which is crested with stone frills and pinnacles. On the wall facing the Piazzetta dei Leoncini the effect is more like that projected by the Miracoli where you can see a great wall of different coloured marbles. The side of the Basilica facing the lagoon, which was once the main entrance on state occasions, is similarly decorated.

The Basilica of St Mark

The interior of the Basilica

Of all the great portals facing Piazza S. Marco, the most interesting is the one on the left (north) which has a 13th-century mosaic scene showing the arrival of the body of St Mark and the Basilica as it then was. This is the only original mosaic left on the Basilica façade. The central portal is interesting for its 13th-century carvings which show Venetian artisans and tradesmen at work. They are very important examples of Italian sculpture of the time.

In the narthex of the Basilica, there are early mosaics on the arches and cupolas, but you need opera glasses to see them properly. On the right, by the entrance to the Zen chapel the oldest and least retouched of the mosaics depicts the *Creation of the World* and on the other three cupolas, the *Story of Joseph* is told.

On the right of the main door, leading from the narthex, you will see the door to a stairway which leads up to the museum and galleries of S. Marco. Here, in room IV of the museum, you can see the original bronze horses which stood on the terrace

facing the Piazza. The horses were first brought to Venice from Constantinople following the Fourth Crusade in the early 13th century and, apart from a spell in Paris in the 19th century when Napoleon kept them, they remained there until the late 1970s. Uninspiring copies now stand in their place to save the originals from the pollution which drifts across from the industrial mainland.

The galleries inside the church provide you with a close up view of the mosaics on the walls and ceiling as well as an exciting bird's-eye view of the whole interior and of the marble floor, the designs on which cannot be appreciated at ground level.

An interesting marble rood screen marks the entrance to the chancel and, if you wish to enter, a fee is expected. Above the screen, you will see the marble figures of Mary, St Mark and the disciples by Jacobello and Pier Paolo dalle Masegne.

To the left of the screen you will see the chapel of the Madonna of Nicopeia where the revered icon is held. This was probably brought from Constantinople during

The replacement horses above the main door

the Fourth Crusade and it is believed to bring good fortune to Venice.

The entrance to the chancel is at the north corner of the screen and if you decide to enter, you will see the *Pala d'Oro* which is a magnificent golden and be-jewelled altarpiece made in Constanti-nople in the 10th century and added to later. This remarkable work is greatly admired for its expert craftwork.

The entry ticket into the Pala d'Oro allows you into the **treasury** which you enter through the south transept. It con-tains a priceless collection of gold and silver, stolen at the sack of Constanti-nople. The **baptistry** lies beside the Treasury but is entered from the south aisle and contains the Gothic tomb of Andrea Dandolo and Sansovino.

S. Marcuola   4 H3
Campo S. Marcuola, Cannaregio. In this 18th-century church by Massari you can find early Tintoretto paintings including the *Last Supper* and a number of marble sculptures by Girolamo Morleiter.

S. Maria Formosa   5 L4
Campo S. Maria Formosa, Castello. The Madonna is said to have appeared to the Bishop of Oderzo and the Bishop was so overcome that he was inspired to build the church of S. Maria Formosa which juts out into the busy campo. The church, which was designed by Codussi, was built with two interesting façades — one facing the canal and the other facing the campo. On the base of its campanile there is a gro-tesque head with an unpleasant expression which shocked Ruskin.

The church is spacious and uncluttered by monuments. The chapel of the Scuola dei Bombardieri displays a fine altarpiece of *St Barbara* by Palma il Vecchio. There is some fine decorative work by Palma il Gio-vane and, in the chapel of the Fruttaroli (fruiterers), there is an altarpiece by Querena.

S. Maria del Giglio   7 J6
Campo S. Maria del Giglio (or Zobenigo), S. Marco. Aesthetes are often repelled by the extravagance of the Baroque style but

this monument to Venetian capitalist, Antonio Barbaro (1680–83) is amusingly theatrical and full of the grand gestures typical of successful businessmen of the time. On the façade, Barbaro is seen surrounded by figures representing the virtues with which he hoped he would be identified. Above and below are the symbols of his material power, the cities where he was administrator and the vessels he commanded.

In the interior of the church, paintings include *The Holy Family* by Rubens and *The Evangelists* by Tintoretto.

S. Maria della Salute   7 J6

When the plague of the early 1630s ended, the people of Venice built the Salute, as it is known, in gratitude. This is one of the most famous churches in Venice and it adds a distinctive beauty to the Canal Grande. Over Longhena's high altar, you will see an excellent sculpture of the *Virgin Casting Out the Plague* by Juste Le Court and there are also works by Tintoretto, Titian, and several others.

There is usually a fee for entry to the Sacristy but you can see some excellent paintings here. The ceiling canvases by Titian of *Cain and Abel*, *The Sacrifice of Isaac* and *David and Goliath* are particularly interesting.

By tradition, the Feast of the Presentation of the Virgin takes place on Nov 21 (see p. 00) when a procession of Venetians and visitors crosses a temporary 'bridge' of boats over the Canal Grande.

S. Moisè   7 K6

Campo S. Moisè, S. Marco. The heavy Baroque façade of S. Moisè was designed by Tremignon and the decoration was carried out by Meyring. The finances for this enterprise were provided by Vincenzo Fini whose bust appears above the central doorway. The interior is equally ornate with 17th and 18th-century paintings of some interest and there is an effective altar front by Roccatagliata. The tombstone of the 18th-century Scottish financial adviser, John Law, is also in the S. Moisè church.

Santa Maria della Salute

S. Pantaleone   7 G5

Campo S. Pantaleone, Dorsoduro. From the outside, this church looks unfinished and not very interesting. The interior is more remarkable, Fumiani's ceiling painting, which took 30 years to complete, shows figures that whirl up into the sky and an intense white light radiates from behind the figure of St Pantaleone. Several chapels are also well decorated with works by Palma il Giovane, Veronese, Antonio Vivarini and Alemagna.

S. Pietro di Castello   9 Q5

Isola di Pietro. This church, on a little island east of Castello, was the Cathedral of the Venetian Republic from the 8th to the 19th century.

There is little of interest in the church itself but the campanile, which Codussi refurbished with Istrian marble, is rather fine.

S. Polo   4 H4

Campo S. Polo, Cannaregio. The church of S. Polo is in the largest campo in Venice where bullfights and masked balls were once held. Inside, you can see paintings by artists such as Tiepolo (father and son), Giambattista, who painted the *Virgin appearing to St John Nepomuk*, and Gian Domenico, who painted the 14 stations of the cross in the chapel under the organ.

S. Salvatore   4 K5

Campo S. Salvatore, S. Marco. The Baroque façade is, at present, being restored but you can visit the splendid Renaissance interior by entering through the Lombard portico in the Merceria. In the right-hand aisle, the third altar is by Sansovino and here you can also see the *Annunciation* by Titian. This was probably one of his last paintings. On the altar of the Luganegheri (The Sausage makers guild) there are statues by Vittoria and an altar piece by Palma il Giovane. The organ doors were painted by Titian's brother Francesco whose frescoes were recently discovered in the sacristy.

The short transepts of the church contain a number of altars and altarpieces and the large tomb of Catarina Cornaro, Queen of Cyprus, in the right transept. Other members of the Cornaro family are on the left.

As you wander around, you will have the opportunity to see the sarcophagus of St Theodore, the former patron of Venice who was replaced by St Mark and, in the left hand chapel, there is the notable *Supper at Emmaus* by Giovanni Bellini. Titian's *Transfiguration* over the high altar is another moving painting which is worthy of your attention.

S. Sebastiano   6 F6

Campo S. Sebastiano, Dorsoduro. This is the church where Veronese made his reputation as a painter and it contains much of his early work including ceiling panels in the sacristy and the nave which he decorated before he was 20 years old. More of his paintings can be seen in the monks choir and over the high altar where there is a picture of the patron saint of the church with the *Virgin in Glory with Sts Catherine, Peter and Francis*. Ten years after his first work at the church, he decorated the main chapel with two magnificent scenes from the life of St Sebastian. Veronese asked to be buried in the church which had played such an important part in his life and he lies near the organ, under a stone bust of him by Carniero.

S. Stae   4 H3

Campo S. Stae, S. Croce. S. Eustachio, (shortened to S. Stae), is a fine example of Baroque style and was built by Domenico Rossi for Doge Alvise Mocenigo. The interior, designed by Grassi, has an interesting collection of paintings by artists who bridged the gap between the High Renaissance and the 18th-century style. Among them were Sebastiano Ricci Piazzetta, Pellegrini, Pittoni and the young Tiepolo whose work developed into the style we now associate with the 18th century.

S. Stefano   6 H5

Campo Francesco Morosini, S. Marco. This is one of the most attractive churches in Venice. It was founded in the 13th century by the hermits of St Augustine and rebuilt in the 14th and 15th centuries.

The warm brick colouring of the church is echoed in the interior where the general spaciousness is broken by two arcades with arches which separate the nave from the aisles. A ship's keel ceiling stretches the whole length of the church to the apse.

On the entrance wall there is a wooden equestrian statue to Domenico Contarini and, to the right, there is an 18th-century sarcophagus by Vittoria and a bust of Senator Zorzi. On the right aisle of the church there is an imposing altar with a painting of the *Birth of the Virgin* by Bambini. At the second altar, there are two statuettes in the style of Tullio Lombardo.

You enter the sacristy by a Renaissance doorway and there are a number of fine works here including three by Tintoretto — *The Last Supper*, *The Washing of the feet* and *Agony in the Garden*. Other paintings of note include the *Baptism of Christ* by Bordone and the *Virgin Mary with child, St Joseph and saints*, which is attributed to Palma il Vecchio. In the left aisle there are two outstanding works — a monument to Surian, who was a physician and philosopher from Rimini, and the Pietro Lombardo statuettes at the side of the tabernacle of the third altar.

The chancel is up three steps over the old crypt. The altar, with its decorated tabernacle is attributed to Alvise Panizza and the figures on each side are probably by Campagna.

S. Zaccaria   8 M5

Campo S. Zaccaria, Castello. One of the most strikingly-decorated churches in Venice with a handsome façade. The lower half, in Gothic style, is by Gambello and the top, by Codussi, is in the Renaissance style. The interior is equally a mixture of Gothic and Renaissance style and its walls are covered from edge to edge with paintings which give the church an enclosed feeling. None of the paintings are real masterpieces except for the Giovanni Bellini *Madonna and Child with Sts Catherine, Peter, Lucy and Jerome* which is a superb altarpiece. In the St Tarsius chapel on the right, there remains part of a mosaic floor from the former church which stood on this site. A 9th-century crypt is below it.

S. Zulian   8 K5

S. Zulian, S. Marco. The church was initially built by Sangovino and was completed by Alessandro Vittoria for the wealthy physician Tommasso Rangone and there is a statue of Rangone on the façade. The interior of this church, which is also known as S. Guilliano, is simple and spacious. The ceiling paintings by Palma il Giovane and Pietro di Mera (Il Fiammingo) relate to St Julian and help to give the church its identity. On the first altar on the right hand wall there is a Veronese *Pietà above three Saints* and on the second there are carvings and statues by Vittoria.

Scalzi   3 F3

Fondamenta Scalzi, Cannaregio. S. Maria di Nazareth, known as Scalzi, was built by Longhena for the barefoot *(scalzi)* brotherhood of the Carmelites in the 17th century. The church has an ornate Baroque façade by Sardi which, like many of the façades of Venetian churches, represents the wealth and self-importance of rich patrons. In this case, it was Gerolamo Cavazza. Although the Tiepolo ceiling (sketches are in the Accademia), which was the church's pride and joy, was destroyed by an Austrian bomb in 1915, there are other examples of the artist's work remaining. Decorations in the interior include the vault painting of *St Theresa in Glory* in the second chapel on the right and the *Agony in the Garden* in the third chapel on the left. The last Venetian doge, Lodovico Manin, is buried in the second chapel.

San Marcuola

CITY SIGHTS

Arsenale   9 N5

Castello. The Arsenale was created in the
12th century by Doge Falier. At the height
of the Republic's fortunes it employed
16,000 ship-building workers and had a
mass production system which could turn
out fully equipped ships in a day. The main
entrance to the walled dock was the land
gate, erected in 1460 by Gambello. Above
the gate, the lion of S. Marco holds an open
book and four Greek lions guard the
entrance. Today the Arsenale is a solitary
and 'ghostly' place populated only by wild
life that rules among the crumbling buildings and rusting iron. It is hoped that, in
the future, parts of the Arsenale can be put
to good use and opened up to the public. At
the moment, you cannot enter, except by
vaporetto (no. 5).

Canal Grande

Venetians call it the Canalazzo; it is about
2¼ mi (3.5 km) long and 230 ft (70 metres)
at its widest point. The only way to see it
properly is from the canal by gondola,
water taxi or vaporetto, preferably by gondola. The trip by gondola takes about an
hour and, on it, you will see most of the
palazzi which belonged to the great patrician families of Venice.

Starting from the Ferrovia or from the
Piazzale Roma, you first go under the
Scalzi bridge. The church of the Scalzi is
on your left and, to the right, you can see S.
Simeone Piccolo with the green dome. The
next major church on your left is S. Geremia, which is by the entrance to the Canal
Cannaregio. S. Marcuola now appears on
the left next to the Palazzo Vendramin
Calerga (the Venice Casino). Opposite,
you will see an oriental-looking palazzo
called the Fondaco dei Turchi which was
in very poor condition for a while and has
been rebuilt, but not to everyone's taste.

The next notable building on the right
is the Baroque church of S. Stae and by

The Arsenale

The Historical Regatta on the Canal Grande

it you will see the Ca' Pesaro (the Gallery of Modern Art and Oriental Museum). Across the canal on the left, you will see the unmistakable Gothic façade of the Ca'd'Oro (Franchetti Museum). The Rialto Bridge lies ahead and on its left is the Fondaco dei Tedeschi — the main German trading headquarters. On the right, you will see the Rialto markets.

After you pass the turmoil around the Rialto you will see the Riva del Carbon on the left where they used to moor the coal barges. The Riva del Vin, where they unloaded wine, is on the right. This area is the heart of the city's business life. The Palazzo Loredan on the left is the Venetian Town Hall. Next to it, you will see the Palazzo Corner where Turner and Thomas Lawrence stayed. The next building is the Palazzo Grimani which is a fine Renaissance building by Sanmichele and it is now used as the Court of Appeal.

Now the canal begins to turn again and the Rio Foscari, which was constructed in the Mussolini era to provide a quick route to the railway station and Piazzale Roma, appears between the Palazzo Balbi, with obelisks on its roof, and the Ca' Foscari.

On the left, on the inner curve of the

canal there are several splendid palazzi — the Ca' Mocenigo owned by the family that provided four doges; Palazzo Contarini with carved lions on the doorway; Palazzo Moro Lin, known as the 'House of the thirteen windows'. Next to it is the imposing Palazzo Grassi (International Centre for Arts and Costume) by Massari who also completed the equally grand Palazzo Rezzonico on the opposite bank.

Ahead lies the Accademia bridge, still in the course of reconstruction at the time of writing. The Accademia art gallery is on the right.

Immediately to the left beyond the bridge you can see the refurbished Palazzo Franchetti. The 15th-century Palazzo Barbaro is next to it. Browning, Monet and Henry James stayed here when it was owned by the Curtis family who bought it in 1852.

The little red house beyond the Palazzo Barbaro is the Casino delle Rose, where Canova had a studio. You will then pass the Ca' Grande, home of the Corner family who objected to a first floor being added to the Palazzo Venier (Guggenheim Collection) on the opposite bank because it would spoil their view.

You now have a spectacular view of the Canal Grande as you approach the Lagoon: on the right you can see the church of S. Maria della Salute and the point of the Dogana. On the left there is a series of de luxe hotels.

Ghetto   1 G2

Cannaregio. In 1516 the ruling Signoria decreed that Venetian Jews should live on an island in the northwest corner of Venice occupied by a metal casting factory. The name 'Ghetto' is derived from the Venetian word for the metal casting factory — *Gettare*. In other cities throughout Europe, the areas in which large Jewish communities lived came to be known as 'Ghettos'. The original Ghetto area, surrounded by the Rio di Ghetto Nuovo and the Rio della Misericordia, became crowded and houses were built higher than in the rest of Venice. Jewish Synagogues were also set up in the area. Some Venetian Jews still live in the Ghetto. The Synagogue and Museum are still there.

Palazzo Ducale (Doge's Palace)   8 L5

The centre of Venetian power between the 9th and the 19th century was focused on the site of the Doge's Palace. Of the original Byzantine building no trace remains but the likelihood is that it was of the traditional castle type with crenellations, fortified towers and drawbridges. The palazzo we see today was, therefore, a revolutionary concept because, here, instead of a fortress, the Venetians built a shimmering pink palazzo with Gothic arches which suggested a confidence in the future not shown by other seats of power of the time.

The new palazzo grew during the 14th and 15th centuries and some of the most important building work was in the Sala del Maggior Consiglio. This hall was designed for important business. All the leading families of Venice had a representative in this hall who voted to pass new laws and elect officials to the government of the Republic.

The names of the architects of the palazzo are not known for certain although it is known that the city architects Piero Baseio and Enrico were involved. What is recorded, however, is that the Sala del Maggior Consiglio was first used in 1419 and that Doge Francisco Foscari was the initiator of much of the decoration of the palazzo. The sculptural decoration of the façades was carried out by Venetian and

A vaporetto on the Canal Grande

Tuscan sculptors who left some superb works of art to posterity but not their names. Sculptures include the *Judgment of Solomon* at the Basilica end of the Piazzetta façade and *Adam and Eve* and the *Drunken Noah* on the front façade. There is a host of lesser sculptures on the capitals of the porticos depicting crusaders, wild beasts, birds and monsters.

The **Porta della Carta,** which is the ceremonial gateway between the palazzo and the Basilica, was designed by Bartolommeo and Giovanni Bon. It was commissioned by Doge Foscari, whose statue appears above the doorway kneeling before the lion of St Mark. Above him, the bust of St Mark is flanked by figures representing the virtues of Venetian government — charity, fortitude, prudence and temperance.

The Porta della Carta leads into the **palace courtyard** which was designed by Antonio Rizzo. He also rebuilt many of the parts of the palazzo destroyed by fire in the 15th century. Next to the courtyard you can see the **Foscari arch** with bronzes of Adam and Eve. Copies of the original stone sculptures by Rizzo are now kept indoors.

In the centre of the courtyard, there are two wells covered with highly ornate bronze lids made by metalworkers at the Arsenale. The clock face next to the Foscari arch was added in the 17th century.

From the entrance to the courtyard, a fine staircase, the **Scala dei Giganti,** by Rizzo rises to the first piano nobile. It is flanked by two large statues of Mercury (some say Mars) and Neptune by Sansovino, representing commerce and seapower which were the two pillars on which Venetian supremacy rested.

The entrance to the Palazzo Ducale lies to the left of the Scala dei Giganti. On the upper floors, rooms are heavily decorated with stucco and paintings designed to impress the visitor with the grandeur and achievements of the Venetian Republic.

From the first floor loggia, Sansovino's **Scala d'Oro** (Golden staircase) climbs to the doges' apartments. One of the rooms in these apartments is the **Sala degli Scarlatti,** the robing room of the magistrates who wore red *(scarlatti)* robes. The fireplace by Tullio and Antonio Lombardo, with the Barbarigo family Coat of Arms, is also of interest in this room.

At the top of the Scala d'Oro you will see the **Atrio Quadrato** (square room) which has a Tintoretto painting of *Justice Presenting the Sword and Scales to Doge Girolamo Priuli* set in a gilded ceiling. The **Sala delle Quattro Porte** (room of the four doors) is next door. This is the waiting room for visitors to the *Signoria* (Senate).

The heavily stuccoed room is named after the ornate doorways in each wall. There is a painting of *Doge Antonio Grimani Before the Faith* which was found in Titian's studio after his death and was probably finished by one of his assistants. Another interesting painting by G. B. Tiepolo portrays *Venice Receiving Homage from Neptune* and there is a painting by Vicentino showing Henry III visiting Venice in 1574.

Ambassadors and leaders of mercenary troops waited in the **Antecollegio** before going in to the Collegio (the cabinet room of the government). The Antecollegio was designed by Palladio and Vittoria and contains fine paintings by Veronese and Tintoretto among others.

The **Sala del Senato,** also known as the Sala dei Pregadi, was used by the doge to invite patricians *(pregare)* to join the Senate. It looks out over the Rio di Palazzo and towards S. Zaccaria which you can see over the tiled roofs. This was the room of the high magistrates of whom there were about 60. Like all the other government bodies, their numbers increased as the Republic grew in power and importance. Here, debates were held on foreign affairs, finance and military matters. Paintings in this room were mainly contributed by Tintoretto and his assistants. One of the best is a fine *Descent from the Cross.* There are also portraits of the doges on the walls with scenes showing the principal events in their lives. There are also a number of paintings by Palma il Giovane.

Adjoining the Sala del Senato on the north side, there is a small chapel and ante chapel. The latter contains drawings of the 18th-century mosaics on the façade of the Basilica.

On the south side, beyond the Sala delle Quattro Porte, you will see the **Sala del Consiglio dei Dieci.** This was the room used by the powerful Council of Ten who controlled the security forces of the State and employed a large group of spies and even assassins to carry out their work. To make the point, the central ceiling painting by Jacopo d'Andrea is entitled *Vice struck down by Job's thunderbolts.* The original painting was by Veronese but, to the Venetian's everlasting chagrin, this was stolen by the French in 1797 and it is now in the Louvre.

At the entrance to the **Sala della Bussola** which is a waiting room just beyond the Sala del Consiglio, you will see the Bocca di Leone, into which letters denouncing citizens of the Republic were posted for investigation by the Council of Ten. People who suspected their neighbours of acts against the state were entitled to make their accusation and put it in the lion's mouth.

The Doge's Palace (Palazzo Ducale)

Maximum security matters were dealt with by three inquisitors, chosen every month from the members of the council. These men sat in their private room in the **Saletta dei Tre Inquisitori.** From here, a stairway leads up to the array of weapons and suits of armour used in defence of the Republic.

From the second piano nobile, a stairway (Scala dei Censori) leads down to a corridor from which you enter the **Sala del Maggior Consiglio.** This was the meeting place of all the Venetian magistrates, an aristocratic body whose names were written in the Libro d'Oro (Golden Book) and who numbered some 1500 or more members. Their meetings were presided over by the doge and the signoria (senate) and it was here that laws were discussed and passed and that decisions were taken about the election of state officials.

Alexander III, thanks to the efforts of Doge Ziani and of the Fourth Crusade led by Doge Dandolo.

All the Doges appear in a frieze along the top of the wall except for Marin Falier whose place is taken by a black banner as he was executed for having dared to try to upset the formal pattern of the government of the Republic.

The Sala del Maggior Consiglio faces the lagoon and most people are glad at this point to stop and enjoy the view towards S. Maria Maggiore.

There is one final room to visit before returning to the world outside and this is the **Sala dello Scrutinio** where elections of officials took place. The hall runs on the Piazzetta side of the palazzo and it is large and imposing with a triumphal arch, called the Peloponnesian arch as it commemorates the victories of Doge Fran-

The Sala del Maggior Consiglio, in the Doge's Palace

The huge hall was, therefore, the centre of democratic opinion such as it was in the Republic. Perhaps in acknowledgment of the ideals of their form of government, there is a huge Tintoretto painting of *Paradise* across the wall behind where the doge sat. This is the largest oil painting in the world and needs to be to hold its own against the incredible array of paintings and moulded stucco that decorate the hall. There are 35 panels of ceiling paintings alone including works by Veronese, Palma il Giovane and Tintoretto and his studio. Paintings covering the walls commemorate such events as the reconciliation between the Emperor Barbarossa and Pope

cisco Morosoni against the Turks. Other victories are celebrated in paintings along the walls and the end wall has a *Last Judgment* by Palma il Giovane. Above the paintings, there is a continuation of the frieze of Doges from the Sala del Maggior Consiglio.

Such an impressive array of architectural and artistic talent leaves many visitors feeling quite stunned. No palace on earth contains such a collection of works of high craftsmanship and, in some cases, genius. One visit is not enough and, as with the Accademia, the only thing to do is to go back again and again to look at what most appeals to you.

Piazza S. Marco   8 K5

The centre of Venetian life for over 1000 years began to assume its present form in the 12th century when the Venetians filled in a canal running in front of the Basilica. The buildings on the right, looking from the Basilica, are the Procuratie Vecchie. These houses belonged to the procurators or magistrates who were the highest power in Venice after the doge. The terrace was built by Codussi with later additions by Bartolommeo Bon, Grigi and Sansovino who was the city architect.

The buildings on the left of the Basilica are the Procuratie Nuove which were begun by Scamozzi in 1586 and completed by Longhena. Napoleon lived here after the fall of the Serenissima and he ordered the building of the Ala Napoleonica to replace the church of S. Germiniano which stood at the west end of the Piazza S. Marco. The Campanile was first built in the 9th century on Roman foundations and it was intended as a watch tower. Its present appearance dates from the 16th century. In 1902 the Campanile fell down into a neat pile of rubble crushing the Loggia under it but harming no one. Some people saw it as a bad omen but exactly 1000 years after it was first built, the Campanile was erected exactly as it had been. You can reach the top by taking the elevator or by climbing a series of ramps with a gentle gradient. The view from the top is stupendous.

The Torre del Orològio (clock tower) was built by Codussi and additions were made by Massari and possibly Lombardo. On the top, there are two figures which strike the giant bell and, because the bronze from which they are made is dark, they have come to be known as the Moors. The clock face tells the hour, phases of the moon and movements of the sun in relation to the signs of the zodiac.

Ponte di Rialto   4 K4

Probably the most famous bridge in Venice, this unusual construction was the first permanent crossing point of the Canal Grande. The views from this bridge are quite spectacular and the area itself is one of the most interesting parts of Venice. If you would like to sample the real Venetian atmosphere, linger for a while at the Rialto markets where you will usually find some good bargains, souvenirs and presents.

The Clock Tower

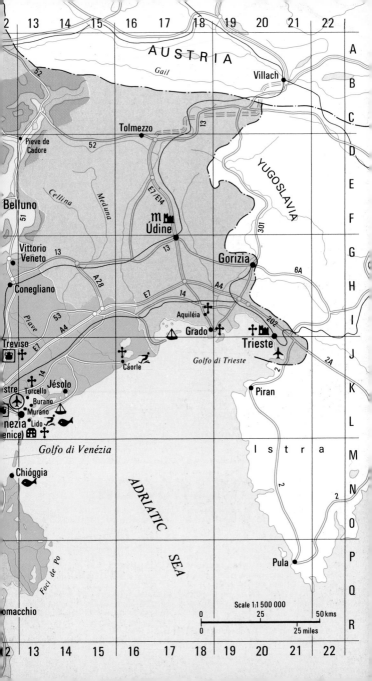

Ponte dei Sospiri   8 L5

The name of this bridge translates as 'Bridge of Sighs'. It leads to the prison and the bridge earned its name because Venetians imagined that prisoners must have sighed sorrowfully as they were led over it to begin their sentences.

Teatro La Fenice   7 J5

S. Marco. The most beautiful theatre in Italy was built by Selva in the 18th century and burned down in 1836. It was rebuilt in the same style and has continued to be the home of great operatic performances. As well as the theatre there are large halls where festivals and concerts are held.

The Bridge of Sighs

THE LAGOON

The Venetian lagoon stretches between the mainland, where the rivers Brenta, Piave and Sile enter, to the sandbanks along the Adriatic. Its length from east to west is 32 mi (52 km). There are some 40 islands in the lagoon, some of them swampy and liable to flooding and others, which were formerly occupied by monasteries or hospitals, are now deserted. The following are those which you are most likely to visit.

Burano

A place of colourful fishermen's houses and good restaurants. Apart from tourism,

the main activities are fishing and lacemaking — an industry which dates back to the 16th century and now survives at the **Scuola dei Merletti** (lace-making school) in Piazza B. Galuppi.

Chióggia

Although it is on the mainland, this fishing village is very much an important feature of the lagoon with a harbour full of fishing boats. The narrow streets with tall houses are very distinctive. As it can be reached by car, its landward side has a great deal of traffic, especially at weekends when the crowds arrive. The duomo by Longhena is

Burano

of some interest and you might care to sample the fresh fish at the restaurants in Corso del Popolo.

Lido 15

The sandy island of the Lido is $7\frac{1}{2}$ mi (12 km) long and has been a fashionable

She sells seashells on the Lido

bathing resort since the 19th century. Smart hotels line the seaside boulevard of Lungomare Gugliemo Marconi and there are many sporting facilities — golf, tennis, horse riding, sailing, surfboarding etc. The Municipal Casino is open in summer (see p. 24) and the big event of the year is the International Film Festival (see p. 31).

Murano   14

The island of Murano has been producing beautifully-crafted glass since the 13th century and the industry is still going strong. Visits to factories are free and you can watch skilful craftsmen doing everything from blowing a small bottle to making a whole chandelier. There is no charge but, if you wish, you can leave a small donation to indicate your pleasure at having watched a demonstration of skills unsurpassed in the making of glassware.

There is a **glass museum** (Museo delle'Arte Vetraria) at Fondamenta Giustinian. A splendid church, the S.S. Maria e Donato, is at Campo S. Donato.

S. Michele   14

The church of S. Michele on this cemetery island is an exquisite little building which is much admired. Diaghilef, Stravinsky and Ezra Pound are buried here.

Giudecca   11-13

This is the largest island outside Venice and was, at one time, the place where patrician Venetians built their villas. It has since declined and is now mainly a site for small industries and home of some impoverished artists but its industrial future looks quite hopeful.

The main architectural feature of Giudecca is the Redentore church by Palladio (see p. 95). The huge Mulino Stucky flour mill was an ambitious 19th-century project which was abandoned in the 1920s and now lies empty.

Torcello

This is the island on which refugees from the mainland first settled in the 5th century. Torcello grew fast until the 14th century when Venice overtook it as the most important power on the lagoon. The only remnant of the original town is the splendid cathedral which was founded in 639 and which has some superb mosaics. The church is S. Fosca, an 11th century building with arcades on three sides.

OUT OF VENICE

At its height, the Venetian Empire stretched over the plain of the *Po* as far as Lombardy. This whole area is now known as the Veneto and it is full of interesting towns and natural beauty spots which are easily reached from Venice. The variety offered by the Veneto could easily fill a whole holiday. For your day-excursions, we have tried to select several of the places which represent different facets of the Veneto treasure trove.

Many of them can be visited by car, train or bus in one day but beware of renting a car for a short period as it can be very expensive.

Aquiléia   I18

(77 mi/124 km from Venice). The village of Aquiléia was an important town in Roman and medieval times. Augustus resided here for a while and the village was a patriarchate of the church. Later, the rise of Venice reduced Aquiléia to a place of little importance.

The remains of its former glory make Aquiléia an interesting place to visit. In its centre you will see the Basilica. It contains a mosaic pavement dating from the time of Theodoric. There is a crypt *(Cripta degli Scavi)* where three levels of mosaics can be seen. Most of the Basilica you see today is the 11th-century church reconstructed from the original one by Bishop Poppo who united the patriarchates of Aquiléia and Grado. The Museo Archeologico in Via Roma contains other Roman and early Christian relics. You can walk around the excavations at Aquiléia passing early Roman houses, Christian Oratories and a market place. The old Roman harbour is to the north of the basilica and what remains of the amphitheatre and Roman baths is to the west.

Asolo   I10

(41 mi/66 km from Venice). This hill town lies northwest of Venice among the Asolean hills which are covered by vineyards and cypresses. In the centre of the town, where Queen Catarina Cornaro of Cyprus lived after she was deposed, there are many old buildings including a duomo with paintings by Lotto and Bassano.

Belluno   F12

(67 mi/108 km from Venice). Belluno is a mountain town above the rivers *Ardo* and *Piave*. In the old town there is a 16th-century duomo designed by Tullio Lombardo and there are paintings by Bassano and Palma il Giovane. Also in the Piazza del Duomo you will see the Renaissance Palazzo dei Rettori and the tower of the castle owned by the former rulers of Belluno.

Brenta Canal

There are many fine villas along the waterways of the *Brenta* as this region was popular among patrician families who escaped from the summer heat and smells to their Palladian villas along the *Brenta*.

An easy way to visit the *Brenta* is by the Burchiello water bus from the S. Marco station near the Zecca, or you can go by bus from the Piazzale Roma which is quicker and gives you more time to visit the villas. Whichever way you go, do not expect to see a typical rural scene all the way as the industrial area has spread into parts of the countryside.

Two of the Brenta villas make an interesting contrast. The Villa Foscari, called Malcontenta, was built by Palladio around 1555 and acquired its nickname because one of the wives of Foscari was banished here and lived out her life in discontent. It is kept in excellent order and its imposing façade is of the type adopted by later imitators of Palladio in England. The interior of the villa is serene and well-proportioned and, in the upper hall and surrounding rooms, there are frescoes by Zelotti and Franco. The villa has a lovely garden.

As you travel in the direction of Padova, you come to **Stra** which is a pleasant town with several villas including the Villa Pisani Nazionale. This grand building has Tiepolo ceilings in the ballroom.

Napoleon bought the Villa Pisani for Josephine's brother, Eugene Beau-harnais and, in our century, Hitler and Mussolini first met here.

Bressanone   A8

(196 mi/315 km from Venice). The town lies off the Bolzano to Brenner Pass *autostrada* where the *Rienza* and *Isarco* rivers meet. Once an independent state, Bressanone fell under the dominion of the Holy Roman Emperors. Henry IV held a council in the baptistry of the duomo to depose Pope Hildebrand. The oldest part of the duomo is the Romanesque cloister which is decorated with 14th and 15th-century frescoes. The town is also an excellent winter sports centre.

Colli Eugánei   M9

The Eugáneian Hills lie to the south of Padova and a number of interesting towns are situated there. The main town is Abano Terme which is a spa, known since Roman times for its power to alleviate rheumatism and arthritis. Today the area is a popular summer holiday resort serving as a good centre for excursions into the hills and to other spas like Montegrotto.

Monselice lies at the southeast corner of the Eugáneian Hills near the *autostrada*. There is a 13th-century castle here with a private museum. If you wish to enter, you should ask at the castle gate.

From Monselice, the road west to Mantua passes the town of Este — home of the Dukes of Este who ruled Ferrara. The

The cloisters in Bressanone

castle at Este now encloses the public garden and the Palazzo Mocenigo inside its crenellated walls. The Palazzo Mocenigo was owned by the family which provide four of Venice's doges. Inside the palazzo, you can visit the Museo Nazionale Atestino which has a collection of antiquities from Roman and earlier times.

The town of Montagnana, which is only a short distance along the Mantua road, is encircled by remarkably well-preserved medieval walls.

The Dolomites

As a change from the flatness of the Lagoon and the plain of the *Po* you may consider going up into the mountains. This is best done by car along the *autostrada* to Verona and then north on the

autostrada to Bolzano. From here, you continue east to Cortina.

You should allow at least two days for this trip and you will be well rewarded. The mountain scenery between Bolzano and Cortina over the Selva, Pordoi and Falzarego Passes is breathtaking. Cortina is just as inspiring. It is surrounded by Dolomite peaks including Monte Cristallo.

On your return, take the road to Titian's birthplace, Pieve de Cadore, and then on to Belluno. An *autostrada* returns you to Venice via Conegliano where you can stop to look at the Cima paintings. You will also pass through Treviso which has a fine duomo and Museo Civico with paintings by Bellini, Bordone and Cima among them.

The Dolomites

Ferrara   Q9

(73 mi/118 km from Venice). This city has often been associated with Venice and was an important medieval city state under the rule of the Dukes of Este. The height of the city's power came in the 13th and 14th centuries when many architects and artists took up residence at the court of the d'Estes and built and decorated the many palaces we enjoy today. The Castello Estense is the main palace in the centre of the city. It has a massive fortress structure surrounded by a moat and

dominates the Piazza della Republica. The castello was begun by Duke Nicolò II and many of its rooms contain the work of early Ferrarese masters such as Bastiniano, Cesare and Filippi. An interesting part of the castello is the chapel of Renée of France who was the wife of Ercole II. Renée was the daughter of Louis XII of France and an ardent Calvinist. She was finally exiled by her husband. In the 16th century, Lucrezia Borgia lived in Ferrara when she was married to Alfonso I.

The Ferrara Duomo lies near the castello. This splendid cathedral was begun by Wiligelmo, sculptor of Modena Cathedral, and has a beautiful façade. The interior of the church was remodelled in the early 18th century but contains many works by artists of the 15th and 16th centuries such as Garófalo, Francia, Guercino and Bastiniano.

Following the Via Voltapaletto, you come to the church of S. Francesco in which there are some fine 16th-century frescoes. Nearby, to the east, the fine Palazzo Schifanoia has a well known series of paintings in the Salone dei Mese by Francesco della Cossa and Ercole Roberti.

The Palazzo dei Diamanti is so called because the walls are covered with the diamond emblem of the d'Este family. There are many excellent works of art in this palazzo. Here, in the Pinacoteca, there is a magnificent collection of works by Ferrarese masters including Cosmè Tura, Francesco di Cossa, Ercole Roberti, Garófalo and Dosso Dossi.

Merano   B6

(188 mi/303 km from Venice). This town, to the northwest of Bolzano, is near the point where the River *Pasini* joins the River *Adige*. It is a mountain resort of ancient origins and has narrow arcaded streets of medieval buildings. Streets are now filled with smart shops that cater to both summer and winter tourists who patronize this delightful resort. Among the old buildings of note are the duomo and a 15th-century castle (Castello Principesco). There is always plenty to do here and the hunting and fishing opportunities are excellent.

Padova   L10

(25 mi/41 km from Venice). Padova has been an important town since the 13th century when its university was founded and the great church of S. Antonio (Il Santo) was first constructed. Today, the busy city traffic flows around three of the world's great masterpieces of architecture, painting and sculpture. The church of Il Santo is a superb building with an exotic Byzantine form which is best appreciated from the cloister. From here, the galleries, minarets and domes form a glorious picture. In the dark church, there are

The Prato del Valle, Padua

The Basilica, Padua

some marvellous sculptures by Donatello around the altar. To see these, you may have to ask the custodian for admittance. In the chapel of S. Antonio (left transept), the bas relief panels are by Sansovino, and Antonio and Tullio Lombardo.

On the Piazza del Santo outside the church you can see one of the world's finest equestrian statues. This one is of Gattamelata (the honeyed cat) who, with Colleoni (who sits upon his horse outside S. Zanipolo in Venice), helped to create the Venetian mainland Empire.

The Capella degli Scrovegni is a small unpretentious building placed amid the few remnants of the Roman arena. The interior of the arena is covered with inspiring early 14th-century Giotto frescoes. Inside the church of the Eremitani (hermits), you will find some excellent frescoes by Montegna and others.

Apart from these exceptional masterpieces, Padova has a number of old churches, museums and medieval streets which require at least a day to visit.

Ravenna   R10

(92 mi/148 km from Venice). Ravenna was first developed by the Emperor Honorius who moved the headquarters of the Roman Empire from Rome to Ravenna in the 5th century. He and his sister, Galla Placida, commissioned the first of the wonderful, mosaic-decorated churches of Ravenna. Their work was carried on by the Ostrogoth Theodoric, and when the Byzantines re-took the city in 540, the evolution and improvement continued under Justinian and his Empress Theodora. Having miraculously survived the ravages of the invaders of the Dark Ages, Ravenna was later destroyed by the French monarch, Louis XII, in the 16th century. However many of the churches survived, some were rebuilt and the mosaics were restored to their former glory.

The earliest work can be seen near the northern city walls at the 6th-century church of S. Vitale which has a Renaissance portal and the interior is of Byzantine design. The marble decoration, mosaics and frescoes were added later in the 16th century.

In the grounds of the church you will see the tomb of Galla Placida, a small cruciform building with magnificent and beautifully-preserved mosaics. From the east end of S. Vitale you can enter the Museo Nazionale, where there are Roman remains and works of art which have been removed from neighbouring churches.

The duomo, which lies to the south of the city, was rebuilt in the 18th century and has a splendid interior decorated with mosaics and sculptural ornaments. The Battistero Neoniano, which is next to the duomo was formerly a Roman bath.

Another great Byzantine church is S. Apollinare Nuovo which was built by Theodoric in the 6th century. There are some superb mosaics above the arches of the Nave walls depicting the *Procession of the Virgin* on one side and the *Martyrs approaching Christ Enthroned* on the other.

Trieste

Above the two main bands of mosaics, there are others showing the Prophets and the *Life of Christ.*

Just south of Ravenna, you can visit the church of S. Apollinare in Classe. The mosaics are mostly in the apse and include the *Transfiguration with Sant'Apollinare,* and *Constantine IV Granting Privileges to the Ravenna Church.* There are also many Greek columns.

Trento   F6

(96 mi/154 km from Venice). Strategically placed in the valley of the *Adige*, Trento has been an important town since Roman times. Caught between the Holy Roman Empire and Papal Italy, the Bishops of Trento learned the art of statesmanship by necessity and became rulers as Bishop-Princes of the independent city until a threat from the Venetian Republic made them turn to the Austrians for help.

The Castello de Buonconsiglio towers above the town. The castello is home of a 13th-century fortress and a Renaissance palace, which is now the Museo Provinciale d'Arte. The custodian accompanies you to the gardens, the Great Hall and other second floor rooms and he also shows you the furnished apartments.

In the town centre the Via Belenzani, which has several fine palazzi, runs from the duomo to the junction with the Via Roma, beyond which there are some

extensive public gardens. You can sit in these gardens watching and appreciating the great mountain ranges that encircle the town.

The 13th-century duomo is a Romanesque marble building of great character. Inside, there are tombs of the powerful bishops.

Trieste   J20

(102 mi/164 km from Venice). An *autostrada* runs all the way from Venice to Trieste which is a busy port near the Yugoslav border. In the centre of the town there is a large castle on top of a hill which was first built by the Venetians in the 12th century and completed by the Austrians in the 16th century when Trieste was their main seaport. The cathedral of S. Giusto, near the castle, contains part of a Roman basilica. There is also a Roman theatre on the slope of the hill.

Údine   G17

(79 mi/127 km from Venice). Udine was a Roman military outpost and then became an independent town until it was taken over by the Venetians in 1420. The centre of the city is Piazza della Libertà dominated by the 15th-century Venetian Gothic Palazzo del Commune. The lion of St Mark stands on a column in the square and there are two huge statues of Hercules and Cacus by sculptors Florean and Ven-

turin, both from Údine. To the north, through the Arco Bollani, you will see the castello. Surrounding old buildings were damaged in the 1976 earthquake. The castle was headquarters of the Venetian governors but now contains the Museo Civico, Museo del Risorgimento and Galleria d'Arte Antica e d'Arte Moderna which includes works by Canova, G. B. Tiepolo, Palma il Giovane and Pordenone. There are many interesting exhibits in this museum.

The duomo, which lies a block away to the south, was begun in the 13th century and finished in the 15th century although it was altered later. The interior is in Baroque style and, in the chapels, there are paintings by Venetian artists. Údine exudes the atmosphere of a mountain town with streams running through it and house fronts occasionally covered with murals.

Verona   L5

(71 mi/115 km from Venice). Although you can visit Verona in one day, it is advisable to allow two as there is much to see in this beautiful city and many of its monuments go back to Roman times. The most impressive remnant from the Roman period is the Arena in Piazza Bra. The inner wall is almost intact and the interior

seating is filled on summer evenings by opera enthusiasts as this is one of the great Italian open air opera houses.

Other Roman remains include the theatre on the hill by the River *Adige*, and the Porta Borsari, which was built during the reign of Claudius.

Medieval times are preserved at the Piazza dei Signori which is surrounded by buildings erected by the della Scala family. This family ruled Verona from 1262 until 1387. Many members of the family are buried in tombs enclosed by an iron fence in a corner of the piazza.

One of the finest medieval buildings is to the west of the town near the Scaligeri castle on the south bank of the *Adige*. This is the church of S. Zeno, which is a remarkable Romanesque building with two towers and a superb bronze door. In the huge interior, which has a ship's keel roof, there is a raised chancel with a marble balustrade and figures of the Apostles above the crypt where S. Zeno is buried.

The most romantic reason for visiting Verona is because it is the town of Romeo and Juliet. Juliet's house, with its famous balcony, is near the lively market at Piazza delle Erbe and her tomb is in the Via del Pontiere where, even if you are sceptical about the legend, you will be moved by the atmosphere of the peaceful cloister.

Juliet's Balcony, Verona

Vicenza   K8

(32 mi/51 km from Venice). Palladio's city is a busy and thriving place dominated by his excellent architecture. In the main square, you will see Palladio's basilica, which was used, not as a church but as a splendid meeting place.

The Corso Palladio runs east to west across Vicenza and, at its western end, there are two more Palladio masterpieces. One is the Palazzo Chericati which faces the river across the Piazza Matteoti and is now home of the Civic Art Gallery. The other is the Teatro Olimpico which is a

magnificent tour de force based on Roman theatre design.

Nearby, the church of S. Corona has Veronese and Giovanni Bellini paintings which are well worth seeing. As you wander from street to street, you will see many other interesting buildings.

More of Palladio's work can be seen outside Vicenza but an overnight stay is recommended if you want to see his great villas. The most famous is the Rotonda, southeast of the city, which he built for Monsignore Almerico. This is a very unusual circular villa. To the east lie the Villa Valmarana, at Lisiera, the Villa Thiene at Quinto, and the Villa Marcello at Bertesina. Each is interesting in its own way and, to the north, the Villa Caldogno, lies unused. The Villa Godi Malinverni on a hill 5 mi (8 km) from Thiene was Palladio's first attempt at villa design. The Villa Piovene on the same hill at a higher level has superb views of the mountains from its large park.

The Vicenza skyline (top), Palladio's Rotunda

INDEX

All place names, buildings and monuments which have a main entry are printed in heavy type. Map references also appear in heavy type and refer to the Venice street maps between pp 32-63.